Recollections Of The Private Life Of Napoleon

Volume 11

by

Louis Constant Wairy

Double9 BOOKS

Recollections Of The Private Life Of Napoleon
Volume 11
by Louis Constant Wairy

ISBN: 978-93-76393-96-1

Published by

DOUBLE 9 BOOKS
2/13-B, Ansari Road
Daryaganj, New Delhi – 110002
info@double9books.com
www.double9books.com
Tel. 011-40042856

ABOUT THE AUTHOR

Louis Constant Wairy is portrayed as an individual whose life path was shaped by early upheaval, eventually leading to a role that placed him in close proximity to a significant leader whose public power contrasted with private complexity. His account reflects a commitment to documenting daily routines, personal habits, and human inconsistencies rather than repeating interpretations influenced by political agendas. Through years of service in an intimate position, he developed insights into the contrast between authority and vulnerability, observing how discipline, ambition, and emotional strain formed an intricate part of the environment surrounding this central figure. His writing emphasizes the value of firsthand experience, using small details and encounters to illuminate aspects of leadership that conventional histories often overlook. Instead of focusing solely on achievements, he highlights the subtler qualities that define private identity, creating a portrayal grounded in observation and shaped by the same tensions between power, responsibility, and humanity that resonate throughout the themes explored in the book.

CONTENTS

CHAPTER XV

During the second day of the battle of Dresden, at the end of which the Emperor had the attack of fever I mentioned in the preceding chapter, the King of Naples, or rather Marshal Murat, performed prodigies of valor. Much has been said of this truly extraordinary prince; but only those who saw him personally could form a correct idea of him, and even they never knew him perfectly until they had seen him on a field of battle. There he seemed like those great actors who produce a complete illusion amid the fascinations of the stage, but in whom we no longer find the hero when we encounter them in private life. While at Paris I attended a representation of the death of 'Hector' by Luce de Lancival, and I could never afterwards hear the verses recited in which the author describes the effect produced on the Trojan army by the appearance of Achilles without thinking of Prince Murat; and it may be said without exaggeration that his presence produced exactly this effect the moment he showed himself in front of the Austrian lines. He had an almost gigantic figure, which alone would have sufficed to make him remarkable, and in addition to this sought every possible means to draw attention to himself, as if he wished to dazzle those who, might have intended to attack him. His regular and strongly marked features, his handsome blue eyes rolling in their orbits, enormous mustaches, and black hair falling in long ringlets over the collar of a kurtka with narrow sleeves, struck the attention at first sight. Add to this the richest and most elegant costume which one would wear even at the theater,—a Polish coat richly embroidered, and encircled by a gilded belt from which hung the scabbard of a light sword, with a straight and pointed blade, without edge and without guard; large amaranth-colored pantaloons embroidered in gold on the seams, and nankeen boots; a large hat embroidered in gold with a border of white feathers, above which floated four large ostrich plumes with an exquisite heron aigrette in the midst; and finally the king's horse, always selected from the strongest and handsomest that could be found, was covered with an elegantly embroidered sky-blue cloth which extended to the ground, and was held in place by a Hungarian or Turkish saddle of the richest workmanship, together with a bridle and stirrups not less magnificent than the rest of the equipment. All these things combined made the King of Naples a being apart, an object of terror and admiration. But what, so to speak, idealized him was his truly chivalrous bravery, often carried to the point of recklessness, as if danger had no existence for him. In truth, this extreme courage was by no means displeasing to the Emperor; and though he perhaps did not always approve of the manner in which it was displayed, his Majesty rarely failed to accord it his praise, especially when he thought necessary to contrast it with the increasing prudence shown by some of his old companions in arms.

On the 28th the Emperor visited the battlefield, which presented a frightful spectacle, and gave orders that everything possible should be done to alleviate the sufferings of the wounded, and also of the inhabitants and peasants who had been ravaged and pillaged, and their fields and houses burned, and then ascended the heights from which he could follow the course of the enemy's retreat. Almost all the household followed him in this excursion. A peasant was brought to him from Nothlitz, a small village where the Emperor Alexander and the King of Prussia had their headquarters during the two preceding days. This peasant, when questioned by the Duke of Vicenza, said he had seen a great personage brought into Nothlitz, who had been wounded the evening before on the staff of the allies. He was on horseback, and beside the Emperor of Russia, at the moment he was struck. The Emperor of Russia appeared to take the deepest interest in his fate. He had been carried to the headquarters of Nothlitz on lances of the Cossacks interlaced, and to cover him they could find only a cloak wet through with the rain. On his arrival at Nothlitz the Emperor Alexander's surgeon came to perform the amputation, and had him carried on an extending chair to Dippoldiswalde, escorted by several Austrian, Prussian, and Russian detachments.

On learning these particulars the Emperor was persuaded that the Prince von Schwarzenberg was the person in question. "He was a brave man," said he; "and I regret him." Then after a silent pause, "It is then he," resumed his Majesty, "who is the victim of the fatality! I have always been oppressed by a feeling that the events of the ball were a sinister omen, but it is very evident now that it was he whom the presage indicated."

While the Emperor gave himself up to these conjectures, and recalled his former presentiments, prisoners who were brought before his Majesty had been questioned; and he learned from their reports that the Prince von Schwarenzberg had not been wounded, but was well, and was directing the retreat of the Austrian grand army. Who was, then, the important personage struck by a French cannonball? Conjectures were renewed on this point, when the Prince de Neuchatel received from the King of Saxony a collar unfastened from the neck of a wandering dog which had been found at Nothlitz. On the collar was written these words, "I belong to General Moreau." This furnished, of course, only a supposition; but soon exact information arrived, and confirmed this conjecture.

Thus Moreau met his death the first occasion on which he bore arms against his native country,—he who had so often confronted with impunity the bullets of the enemy. History has judged him severely; nevertheless, in spite of the coldness which had so long divided them, I can assert that the Emperor did not learn without emotion the death of Moreau, notwithstanding his indignation that so celebrated a French general could have taken up arms against France, and worn the Russian cockade. This unexpected death produced an evident effect in both camps, though our soldiers saw in it only a just judgment from Heaven, and an omen favorable to the Emperor. However that may be, these are the particulars, which I learned a short time after, as they were related by the valet de chambre of General Moreau.

The three sovereigns of Russia, Austria, and Prussia had been present on the 27th at the battle on the heights of Nothlitz, but had retired as soon as they saw that the battle was lost. That very day General Moreau was wounded by a cannon-ball near the intrenchments in front of Dresden, and about four o'clock in the afternoon was conveyed to Nothlitz, to the country house of a merchant named Salir, where the Emperors of Austria and Russia had established their headquarters. Both limbs of the general were amputated above the knee. After the amputation, as he requested something to eat and a cup of tea, three eggs were brought him on a plate; but he took only the tea. About seven o'clock he was placed on a litter, and carried to Passendorf by Russian soldiers, and passed the night in the country house of M. Tritschier, grand master of forests. There he took only another cup of tea, and complained greatly of the sufferings he endured. The next day, the 28th of August, at four o'clock in the morning, he was conveyed, still by Russian soldiers, from Passendorf to Dippodiswalde, where he took a little white bread and a glass of lemonade at the house of a baker named Watz. An hour after he was carried nearer to the frontiers of Bohemia, borne by Russian soldiers in the body of a coach taken off the wheels. During the entire route he incessantly uttered cries which the extremity of his sufferings drew from him.

These are the details which I learned in regard to Moreau; and, as is well known, he did not long survive his wound. The same ball which broke both his legs carried off an arm from Prince Ipsilanti, then aide-de-camp to the Emperor Alexander; so that if the evil that is done can be repaired by the evil received, it might be said that the cannon-shot which tore away from us General Kirgener and Marshal Duroc was this day sent back on the enemy. But alas! it is a sad sort of consolation that is drawn from reprisals.

It may be seen from the above, and especially from the seemingly decisive benefits arising from the battle of Dresden, that since the resumption of hostilities, in every place where our troops had been sustained by the all-powerful presence of the Emperor, they had obtained successes; but unfortunately this was not the case at points distant from the main line of operations. Nevertheless, seeing the allies routed by the army which he commanded in person, and certain, moreover, that General Vandamme had held the position which he had indicated to him through General Haxo, his Majesty returned to his first idea of marching on Berlin, and already even had disposed his troops with this intention, when the fatal news arrived that Vandamme, the victim of his own rashness, had disappeared from the field of battle, and his ten thousand men, surrounded on all sides, and overwhelmed by numbers, had been cut to pieces. It was believed that Vandamme was dead, and it was not until later we learned that he had been taken prisoner with a part of his troop. It was learned also that Vandamme, incited by his natural intrepidity, and unable to resist a desire to attack the enemy whom he saw within his grasp, had left his intrenchments to make the attack. He had conquered at first, but when after his victory he attempted to resume his former position he found it occupied, as the Prussians had seized it; and though he fought with all the abandon of despair, it was all in vain, and General Kleist, proud of this fine trophy, conducted him in triumph to Prague. It was while speaking of this audacious attack of Vandamme that the Emperor used this expression, which has been so justly admired, "For a retreating enemy it is necessary to make a bridge of gold, or oppose a wall of brass." The Emperor heard with his usual imperturbability the particulars of the loss he had just experienced, but nevertheless repeatedly expressed his astonishment at the deplorable recklessness of Vandamme, and said he could not comprehend how this experienced general could have allowed himself to be drawn away from his position. But the deed was done, and in such instances the Emperor never lost time in useless recriminations. "Come," said he, addressing the Duke of Bassano, "you have just heard—that means war from early in the morning until late in the evening."

After giving various orders to the army and his chiefs, the Emperor left Dresden on the evening of the 3d of September, with the intention of regaining what he had lost from the audacious imprudence of General Vandamme. But this defeat, the first we had sustained since the resumption of hostilities, became the forerunner of the long series of reverses which awaited us. It might have been said that victory, having made one last effort in our favor at Dresden, had finally grown weary; for the remainder of the campaign was but a succession of disasters, aggravated by treachery of every description, and ending in the horrible catastrophe at Leipzig. Before leaving Dresden we had learned of the desertion to the enemy of a Westphalian regiment, with arms and baggage.

The Emperor left Marshal Saint-Cyr in Dresden with thirty thousand men, with orders to hold it to the last extremity, since the Emperor wished to preserve this capital at any price. The month of September was spent in marches and countermarches around this city, with no events of decided importance. Alas! the Emperor was never again to see the garrison of Dresden. Circumstances becoming still more embarrassed, imperiously demanded that his Majesty should promptly oppose some obstacle to the progress of the allies. The King of Saxony, furnishing an example of fidelity rare among kings, determined to accompany the Emperor, and entered his carriage in company with the queen and the Princess Augusta, having the headquarters' staff as escort. Two days after his departure the Saxon troops joined the French army at Eilenburg, on the banks of the Mulda. The Emperor exhorted these allies, whom he believed faithful, to maintain the independence of their country, pointed out to them how Prussia was threatening Saxony, and endeavoring to acquire her most beautiful provinces, and reminded them of the proclamation of their sovereign, his worthy and faithful ally; finally he spoke to them in the name of military honor, urging them, in closing, to take it always as their guide, and to show themselves worthy rivals of the soldiers of the grand army with whom they had made common cause, and beside whom they were now about to fight. The words of the Emperor were translated and repeated to the Saxons by the Duke of Vicenza; and this language from the lips of one whom they regarded as the friend of their sovereign and the saviour of their capital seemed to produce a profound impression. The march was then begun in confidence, with no premonition of the approaching defection of these very men who had so often greeted the Emperor with their cries of enthusiasm, swearing to fight to the death rather than abandon him.

His Majesty's plan then was to fall on Blucher and the Prince Royal of Sweden, from whom the French army was separated only by a river. We therefore left Eilenburg, where the Emperor parted with the King of Saxony and his family, the Duke of Bassano, the grand park of artillery, and all the conveyances, and directed our course towards Duben. Blucher and Bernadotte had retired, leaving Berlin uncovered. Then the Emperor's plans became known; and it was seen that he was marching on Berlin, and not on Leipzig, and that Diiben was only the meeting-place for the various corps, who, when united, were to march on the capital of Prussia, which the Emperor had already seized twice.

The time was unfortunately past when a simple indication of the Emperor's plans was regarded as a signal of victory. The chiefs of the army, who had until now been perfectly submissive, began to reflect, and even took the liberty of disapproving of plans which they were afraid to execute. When the army became aware of the Emperor's intention to march on Berlin, it was the signal for almost unanimous discontent. The generals who had escaped the disasters of Moscow, and the dangers of the double campaign in Germany, were fatigued, and perhaps eager to reap the benefits of their good fortune, and at last to enjoy repose in the bosom of their families. A few went so far as to accuse the Emperor of being anxious to still extend the war. "Have there not been enough killed?" said they, "Must we all share the same fate?" And these complaints were not kept for secret confidences, but were uttered publicly, and often even loud enough to reach the ears of the Emperor; but in that case his Majesty seemed not to hear.

Amidst this disaffection of a large number of the chiefs of the army, the defection of Bavaria was learned, and gave an added strength to the anxiety and discontent inspired by the Emperor's resolution; and then occurred what had never taken place before: his staff united their entreaties that he should abandon his plans in regard to Berlin, and march on Leipzig. I saw how much the Emperor suffered from the necessity of listening to such remonstrances, notwithstanding the respectful language in which they were couched. For two entire days his Majesty remained undecided; and how long these forty-eight hours were! Never did abandoned cabin or bivouac present a more mournful sight than the sad chateau of Duben. In this doleful residence I saw the Emperor for the first time entirely unemployed; the indecision to which he was a prey absorbed him so entirely that his character seemed entirely changed. Who could believe it? To the activity which drove him on, and, so to speak, incessantly devoured him, had succeeded a seeming indifference which is perfectly indescribable. I saw him lie on the sofa nearly a whole day, the table before him covered with maps and papers at which he did not even glance, and with no other occupation for hours than slowly tracing large letters on sheets of white paper. This was while he was vacillating between his own will and the entreaties of his generals. At the end of two days of most painful suspense he yielded; and from that time all was lost. How much better it would have been had he not listened to their complaints, but had again allowed himself to be guided by the presentiments which possessed him! He repeated often, with grief, while recalling the concessions he made at that time, "I should have avoided many disasters by continuing to follow my own impulses; I failed only by yielding to those of others."

The order for departure was given; and as if the army felt as much pride in triumphing over the will of its Emperor as they would have felt in beating the enemy by obeying the dictates of his genius, they abandoned themselves to outbursts of joy which were almost beyond reason. Every countenance was radiant. "We shall now," they repeated on all sides, "we shall now see France again, embrace our children, our parents, and our friends!" The Emperor and Marshal Augereau alone did not share the general light-heartedness. The Duke of Castiglione had just arrived at headquarters, after having in some measure avenged on the army of Bohemia, Vandamme's defeat. He, like the Emperor, had dark presentiments as to the consequences of this retrograde movement, and knew that desertions on the way would add to the number of the enemy, and were so much the more dangerous since these deserters had so recently been our allies and knew our positions. His Majesty yielded with a full conviction of the evil which would result; and I heard him at the end of a conversation with the marshal which had lasted more than an hour, utter these words, "They would have it so."

The Emperor on his march to Duben was at the head of a force which might be estimated at one hundred and twenty-five thousand men. He had taken this direction with the hope of finding Blucher again on the Mulda; but the Prussian general had recrossed the river, which contributed much to give credit to a rumor which had been circulated for some time. It was said that in a council of the allied sovereigns held recently at Prague, and at which Moreau and the Prince Royal of Sweden were present, it had been agreed that as far as possible they should avoid engaging in a battle whenever the Emperor commanded his army in person, and that operations should be directed only against smaller bodies commanded by his lieutenants. It is impossible, certainly, to render more striking homage to the superiority of the Emperor's genius; but it was at the same time stopping him in his glorious career, and paralyzing his usually all- powerful action.

However that may be, the evil genius of France having obtained the ascendency over the good genius of the Emperor, we took the road to Leipzig, and reached it early on the morning of the 15th of October. At that very moment the King of Naples was in the midst of an engagement with the Prince von Schwarzenberg; and his Majesty, on hearing the sound of cannon, crossed the town, and visited the plain where the engagement was taking place. On his return he received the royal family of Saxony, who had come to join him. During his short stay at Leipzig, the Emperor performed an act of clemency which must undoubtedly be considered most meritorious if we take into consideration the gravity of the circumstances in which we were placed. A merchant of this city named Moldrecht was accused and convicted of having distributed among the inhabitants, and even in the army, several thousand copies of a proclamation in which the Prince Royal of Sweden invited the Saxons to desert the cause of the Emperor. When arraigned before a tribunal of war, M. Moldrecht could not exculpate himself; and, indeed, this was an impossibility, since several packages of the fatal proclamation had been found at his residence. He was condemned to death, and his family in deep distress threw themselves at the feet of the King of Saxony; but, the facts being so evident and of such a nature that no excuse was possible, the faithful king did not dare to grant indulgence for a crime committed even more against his ally than against himself. Only one recourse remained for this unhappy family, which was to address the Emperor; but as it was difficult to reach him, M. Leborgne D'Ideville, interpreting secretary, was kind enough to undertake to place a note on the Emperor's desk, who after reading it ordered a postponement which was equivalent to a full pardon. Events followed in their course, and the life of M. Moldrecht was saved.

Leipzig, at this period, was the center of a circle in which engagements took place at numerous points and almost incessantly. Engagements lasted during the days of the 16th, 17th, and 18th; and his Majesty, as a poor return for his clemency towards M. Moldrecht, reaped the bitter fruits of the proclamation which had been scattered in every direction through the efforts of this merchant. On that day the Saxon army deserted our cause, and reported to Bernadotte. This left the Emperor a force of only one hundred and ten thousand men, with an opposing force of three hundred and thirty thousand; so that if when hostilities were resumed we were only as one to two, we were now only one to three. The day of the 18th was, as is well known, the fatal day. In the evening the Emperor, seated on a folding stool of red morocco in the midst of the bivouac fires, was dictating to the Prince of Neuchatel his orders for the night, when two commanders of artillery were presented to his Majesty, and gave him an account of the exhausted condition of the ammunition chests. In five days we had discharged more than two hundred thousand cannon-balls, and the ammunition being consequently exhausted there was barely enough left to maintain the fire for two hours longer; and as the nearest supplies were at Madgeburg and Erfurt, whence it would be impossible to obtain help in time, retreat was rendered absolutely necessary.

Orders were therefore given for a retreat, which began next day, the 19th, at the end of a battle in which three hundred thousand men had engaged in mortal combat, in a confined space not more than seven or eight leagues in circumference. Before leaving Leipzig, the Emperor gave to. Prince Poniatowski, who had just earned the baton of a marshal of France, the defense of one of the faubourgs. "You will defend the faubourg on the south," said his Majesty to him. "Sire," replied the prince, "I have very few men."—"You will defend it with those you have." "Ah, Sire, we will remain; we are all ready to die for your Majesty." The Emperor, moved by these words, held out his arms to the prince, who threw himself into them with tears in his eyes. It was really a farewell scene, for this interview of the prince with the Emperor was their last; and soon the nephew of the last king of Poland found, as we shall soon see, a death equally as glorious as deplorable under the waves of the Elster.

[Prince Joseph Anthony Poniatowski, born at Warsaw, 1762. Nephew of Stanislas Augustus, the last king of Poland. He commanded the Polish army against Russia, 1792, and served under Kosciuszko, 1794. He led an army of Poles under Napoleon, 1807 and 1809, and commanded a corps in the Russian campaign. Had Napoleon succeeded in that campaign, Poniatowski would have been made king of Poland. Wounded, and made a marshal at Liepzig, he was drowned on the retreat.]

At nine o'clock in the morning the Emperor took leave of the royal family of Saxony. The interview was short, but distressing and most affectionate on the part of each.

The king manifested the most profound indignation at the conduct of his troops. "I could never have imagined it," said he; "I thought better of my Saxons; they are only cowards;" and his grief was so intense that the Emperor, notwithstanding the immense disadvantage which had accrued to him from the desertion of the Saxons during the battle, sought to console this excellent prince.

As his Majesty urged him to quit Leipzig in order that he might not be exposed to the dangers attending the capitulation which had now become absolutely necessary, this venerable prince replied, "No; you have already done enough, and it is carrying generosity too far to risk your person by remaining a few minutes longer in order to console us." Whilst the King of Saxony was expressing himself thus, the sound of heavy firing of musketry was heard, and the queen and Princess Augusta joined their entreaties to those of the monarch, in their excessive fright already seeing the Emperor taken and slain by the Prussians. Some officers entered, and announced that the Prince Royal of Sweden had already forced the entrance of one of the faubourgs; that General Beningsen, General Blucher, and the Prince von Swarzenberg were entering the city on every side; and that our troops were reduced to the necessity of defending themselves from house to house, and the Emperor was himself exposed to imminent peril. As there was not a moment to lose, he consented at. last to withdraw; and the King of Saxony escorted him as far as the foot of the palace staircase, where they embraced each other for the last time.

CHAPTER XVI

It was exceedingly difficult to find an exit from Leipzig, as this town was surrounded on every side by the enemy. It had been proposed to the Emperor to burn the faubourgs which the heads of the columns of the allied armies had reached, in order to make his retreat more sure; but he indignantly rejected this proposal, being unwilling to leave as a last adieu to the King of Saxony his cities abandoned to the flames. After releasing him from his oath of fidelity, and exhorting him to now consider only his own interests, the Emperor left him, and directed his course to the gate of Ramstadt; but he found it so encumbered that it was an impossibility to clear a passage, and he was compelled to retrace his steps, again cross the city, and leave it through the northern gate, thus regaining the only point from which he could, as he intended, march on Erfurt; that is, from the boulevards on the west. The enemy were not yet completely masters of the town, and it was the general opinion that it could have been defended much longer if the Emperor had not feared to expose it to the horrors of a siege. The Duke of Ragusa continued to offer strong resistance in the faubourg of Halle to the repeated attacks of General Blucher; while Marshal Ney calmly saw the combined forces of General Woronzow, the Prussian corps under the orders of General Billow, and the Swedish army, break themselves to pieces against his impregnable defenses.

So much valor was nevertheless at last compelled to yield to numbers, and above all to treachery; for at the height of the combat before the gates of Leipzig, a battalion from Baden, which until then had fought valiantly in the French ranks, suddenly abandoned the gate Saint-Peter, which it was commissioned to defend, and at the entrance to the city gave itself up to the enemy. Thereupon, according to what I have heard related by several officers who were in this terrible tumult, the streets of Leipzig presented a most horrible sight; and our soldiers, now compelled to retire, could do so only by disputing every step of the ground. An irreparable misfortune soon filled the Emperor's soul with despair.

I shall now relate the events which signalized this deplorable day just as my memory recalls them. I do not know to what cause to attribute it, but none of the many stirring events which I witnessed present themselves more distinctly before my mind than a scene which took place under the walls of Leipzig. Having triumphed over incredible obstacles, we at last succeeded in crossing the Elster on the bridge at the mill of Lindenau. I can still see the Emperor as he stationed officers along the road charged to indicate to stragglers where they might rejoin their respective commands. On this day, after the immense loss sustained owing to a disparity of numbers, he showed the same solicitude concerning everything as after a decisive triumph. But he was so overcome by fatigue that a few moments of sleep became absolutely necessary, and he slept profoundly under the noise of the cannon which thundered around him on all sides. Suddenly a terrible explosion occurred, and a few moments after the King of Naples entered his Majesty's barrack accompanied by Marshal Augereau. They brought sad news-the great bridge over the Elster had just been blown up. This was the last point of communication with the rear guard, which consisted of twenty thousand men now left on the other side of the river under the command of Marshal Macdonald. "This, then, is how my orders are executed!" exclaimed the Emperor, clasping his head between his hands. He remained a moment buried in thought and absorbed in his own reflections.

The fact was, his Majesty had given orders to undermine all the bridges over the Elster and have them blown up, but not until after the French army had crossed the river in safety. I have since heard this event discussed from many points of view, and have read many contradictory accounts. It is not my province to shed light on a point of history which forms such a subject of controversy, and I have consequently limited myself to relating as I have done only what came within my own knowledge. Nevertheless, I may be permitted to make to my readers one simple observation which presents itself to my mind whenever I read or hear it said that the Emperor himself had the bridge blown up in order to shelter himself from the enemy's pursuit. I ask pardon for such an expression, but this supposition appeared to me an absurdity so incredible as to surpass belief; for it is very evident that if under these disastrous circumstances he could think only of his own personal safety, he would not a short time before have voluntarily prolonged his stay in the palace of the King of Saxony, where he was exposed to much more imminent danger than he could have encountered after leaving Leipzig. Moreover, the Emperor was far from enjoying the consternation which struck him when he learned that twenty thousand of his brave soldiers were separated from him perhaps forever.

How many misfortunes were the inevitable results of the destruction of the last bridge on the road from Leipzig to Lindenau! And how many deeds of heroism, the greater part of which will remain forever unknown, mark this disaster! Marshal Macdonald, seeing himself separated from the army, plunged on horseback into the Elster, and was fortunate enough to reach the other bank; but General Dumortier, attempting to follow his intrepid chief, disappeared and perished in the waves with a great number of officers and soldiers; for all had sworn not to surrender themselves to the enemy, and it was only a small number who submitted to the cruel necessity of being made prisoners. The death of Prince Poniatowski caused intense sorrow in the heart of the Emperor; and it may be said that every one at headquarters was deeply distressed at the loss of our Polish hero, and all were eager to learn the particulars of so grievous and irreparable a misfortune. As was well known, his Majesty had given him orders to cover the retreat of the army, and all felt that the Emperor could not have bestowed this trust more worthily. It is related that seeing himself pressed by the enemy against the bank of the river, with no means of crossing, he was heard to say to those around him, "Gentlemen, here we must die with honor!" It is added that putting into practice this heroic resolution he swam across the waters of the Pleisse in spite of the wounds he had received in the stubborn combat he had sustained since morning. Then finding no longer any refuge from inevitable captivity, except in the waters of the Elster, the brave prince had thrown himself into it without considering the impassable steepness of the opposite bank, and in a few moments he with his horse was ingulfed beneath the waves. His body was not found until five days afterwards, and then drawn from the water by a fisherman. Such was the end, both deplorable and glorious, of one of the most brilliant and chivalrous of officers, who showed himself worthy to rank among the foremost French generals. Meanwhile the lack of ammunition compelled the Emperor to retire promptly, although in remarkably good order, to Erfurt, a town well furnished with both provisions and forage, as well as material for arming and equipping the army,—in fact with all the materials of war. His Majesty arrived on the 23d, having engagements each day, in order to protect his retreat against forces four or five times as numerous as those remaining at his disposal. At Erfurt the Emperor remained only two days, and left on the 25th after bidding adieu to his brother-in-law the King of Naples, whom he was never to see again. I witnessed a part of this last interview, and remarked a certain constraint in the manner of the King of Naples, which, however, his Majesty seemed not to perceive. It is true that the king did not announce his immediate departure, and his Majesty was ignorant that this prince had secretly received an Austrian general.

> [This was Count Mier, charged to guarantee to Murat the possession of his kingdom if he abandoned the cause of the Emperor. He abandoned him. What did he gain?—NOTE BY THE EDITOR.]

His Majesty was not informed of this until afterwards, and manifested little surprise. Moreover (I call attention to this because I so often had occasion to remark it), so many severe blows repeated in such quick succession had struck the Emperor for some time past, that he seemed to have become almost insensible, and it might well have been said that he felt himself perfectly intrenched in his ideas of fatality. Nevertheless, his Majesty, though unmoved under his own misfortunes, gave full vent to his indignation on learning that the allied sovereigns considered the King of Saxony as their prisoner, and had declared him a traitor, simply because he was the only one who had not betrayed him. Certainly if fortune had again become favorable to him, as in the past, the King of Saxony would have found himself master of one of the most extensive kingdoms of Europe; but fortune was hereafter to be always adverse, and even our victories brought us only a barren glory.

Thus, for instance, the French army soon covered itself with glory at Hanau, through which it was necessary to pass by overwhelming the immense army of Austrians and Bavarians collected at this point under the command of General Wrede. Six thousand prisoners were the result of this triumph, which at the same time opened to us the road to Mayence, which we expected to reach without other obstacles. It was on the 2d of November, after a march of fourteen days from Leipzig, that we again beheld the banks of the Rhine, and felt that we could breathe in safety.

Having devoted five days to reorganizing the army, giving his orders, and assigning to each of the marshals and chiefs of the several corps the post he was to occupy during his absence, the Emperor left Mayence on the 7th, and on the 9th slept at Saint-Cloud, to which he returned preceded by a few trophies, as both at Erfurt and Frankfort we had taken twenty banners from the Bavarians. These banners, presented to the minister of war by M. Lecouteux aide-de-camp to the Prince de Neuchatel, had preceded his Majesty's arrival in Paris by two days, and had already been presented to the Empress, to whom the Emperor had done homage in the following terms:

"MADAME, AND MY VERY DEAR WIFE,—

> I send you twenty banners taken by my army at the battles of Wachau, Leipzig, and Hanau. This is an homage it gives me pleasure to render to you. I desire that you will accept it as a mark of my entire satisfaction with the manner in which you have administered the regency which I confided to you."

Under the Consulate and during the first six years of the Empire, whenever the Emperor had returned to Paris after a campaign, it was because that campaign was finished, and the news of a peace concluded in consequence of a victory had always preceded him. For a second time he returned from Mayence under different circumstances. In this case, as on the return from Smorghoni, he left the war still in progress, and returned, not for the purpose of presenting to France the fruit of his victories, but to demand new subsidies of men and money in order to repair the defeat and losses sustained by our army. Notwithstanding this difference in the result of our wars, the welcome accorded to his Majesty by the nation was still the same, apparently at least; and the addresses by the different towns of the interior were not less numerous, nor less filled with expressions of devotion; and those especially who were the prey of fears for the future showed themselves even more devoted than all others, fearing lest their fatal premonitions should be discovered. For my own part, it had never occurred to me that the Emperor could finally succumb in the struggle he was maintaining; for my ideas had never reached this point, and it is only in reflecting upon it since that I have been able to comprehend the dangers which threatened him at the period we had now reached. He was like a man who had passed the night on the edge of a precipice, totally unaware of the danger to which he was exposed until it was revealed by the light of day. Nevertheless, I may say that every one was weary of the war, and that all those of my friends whom I saw on the return from Mayence spoke to me of the need of peace.

Within the palace itself I heard many persons attached to the Emperor say the same thing when he was not present, though they spoke very differently in the presence of his Majesty. When he deigned to interrogate me, as he frequently did, on what I had heard people say, I reported to him the exact truth; and when in these confidential toilet conversations of the Emperor I uttered the word peace, he exclaimed again and again, "Peace! Peace! Ah! who can desire it more than I? There are some, however, who do not desire it, and the more I concede the more they demand."

An extraordinary event which took place the very day of his Majesty's arrival at Saint-Cloud, when it became known, led to the belief that the allies had conceived the idea of entering upon new negotiations. In fact, it was learned that M. de Saint-Aignan, his Majesty's minister at the ducal court of Saxony, had been taken by main force and conducted to Frankfort, where were then assembled M. de Metternich, the Prince von Schwarzenberg, and the ministers of Russia and Prussia. There overtures entirely in the interests of peace were made to him on the part of the allied sovereigns, after which M. de Saint-Aignan was allowed to return immediately to the Emperor to inform him of the details of his seizure and the propositions which had been made to him. These offers made by the allies, of which I was not informed, and consequently can say nothing, seemed to strike the Emperor as worthy of consideration; and there was soon a general rumor in the palace that a new Congress was to be assembled at Manheim; that the Duke of Vicenza had been appointed by his Majesty as minister plenipotentiary; and that in order to give more dignity to his mission, the portfolio of foreign affairs had been at the same time committed to him. I remember that this news revived the hopes of all, and was most favorably received; for although it was doubtless the effect of prejudice, no one could be ignorant that the general public did not see with pleasure the Duke of Bassano in the place to which the Duke of Vicenza was called to succeed him. The Duke of Bassano was said to have acted in accordance with what he believed to be the secret wishes of the Emperor, and to be averse to peace. It will be seen later, by an answer which his Majesty made to me at Fontainebleau, how groundless and without foundation were these rumors. It seemed then exceedingly probable that the enemy really intended to treat for peace; since in procuring openly by force a French negotiator, they had forestalled any credit which might accrue to the Emperor from making overtures for peace.

What above all gave great weight to the general belief in the disposition of Europe towards peace was that not simply a Continental peace was in question as at Tilsit and Schoenbrunn, but also a general peace, in which England was to enter as a contracting party; so that in consequence it was hoped that the gain in the permanence of such peace would offset the severity of its terms. But unfortunately this hope, which was indulged with the joy of anticipation, lasted only a short time; and it was soon learned that the propositions made to M. de Saint-Aignan were only a bait, and an old diplomatic ruse which the foreigners had made use of simply in order to gain time by deluding the Emperor with vain hopes. In fact, a month had not passed away, there had not even been time to complete the preliminary correspondence usual in such cases, when the Emperor learned of the famous declaration of Frankfort, in which, far from entering into negotiations with his Majesty, it was attempted to separate his cause from that of France. What a mass of intrigues! Let one bless with a thankful heart his mediocrity when he compares himself with men condemned to live amid this labyrinth of high impostures and honorable hypocrisies! A sad certainty was obtained that the foreigners wished a war of extermination, and renewed consternation ensued where hope had begun to reign; but the genius of his Majesty had not yet deserted him, and from this time all his efforts were directed towards the necessity of once again meeting the enemy face to face, no longer in order to conquer his provinces, but to prevent an invasion of the sacred soil of his own country.

CHAPTER XVII

In speaking of the year 1813, an account of the incredible number of affiliations which took place at this time between secret societies recently formed in Italy and Germany should not be omitted. The Emperor from the time when he was only First Consul, not only did not oppose the opening of Masonic lodges, but we have every reason to believe secretly favored them. He was very sure that nothing originated in these meetings which could be dangerous to his person or injurious to his government; since Freemasonry counted among its votaries, and even had as chiefs, the most distinguished personages of the state. Moreover, it would have been impossible in these societies, where a few false brethren had slipped in, for a dangerous secret, had there been one, to escape the vigilance of the police. The Emperor spoke of it sometimes as pure child's play, suitable to amuse idlers; and I can affirm that he laughed heartily when told that the archchancellor, in his position as chief of the Grand Orient, had presided at a Masonic banquet with no less dignity than would have comported with the presidency of the senate or of the council of state. Nevertheless, the Emperor's indifference did not extend to societies known in Italy under the name of Carbonari, and in Germany under various titles. We must admit, in fact, that since the undertakings of two young Germans initiated in Illuminism, it was natural that his Majesty should not have seen without anxiety the propagation of those bonds of virtue in which young fanatics were transformed into assassins.

I know nothing remarkable in relation to the Carbonari, since no circumstance connected our affairs with those of Italy. In regard to the secret societies of Germany, I remember that during our stay at Dresden I heard them mentioned with much interest, and not without fears for the future, by a Saxon magistrate with whom I had the honor of associating frequently. He was a man about sixty years of age, who spoke French well, and united in the highest degree German stolidity with the gravity natural to age. In his youth he had lived in France, and part of his education had been received at the College of Soreze; and I attributed the friendship which he showed for me to the pleasure he experienced in conversing about a country the memory of which seemed very dear to him. I remember perfectly well to-day the profound veneration with which this excellent man spoke to me of one of his former professors of Soreze, whom he called Don Ferlus; and I must have had a defective memory indeed had I forgotten a name which I heard repeated so often.

My Saxon friend was named M. Gentz, but was no relation of the diplomat of the same name attached to the Austrian chancellery. He was of the Reformed religion, very faithful in the performance of his religious duties; and I can assert that I never knew a man with more simple tastes, or who was more observant of his duties as a man and a magistrate. I would not like to risk saying what were his inmost thoughts concerning the Emperor; for he rarely spoke of him, and if he had anything unpleasant to say it may be readily understood that he would not have chosen me as his confidant. One day when we were together examining the fortifications which his Majesty had erected at many points on the left bank of the Elbe, the conversation for some reason happened to fall on the secret societies of Germany, a subject with which I was perfectly unacquainted. As I was questioning him in order to obtain information, M. Gentz said to me, "It must not be believed that the secret societies which are multiplying in Germany in such an extraordinary manner have been protected by the sovereigns; for the Prussian government sees them grow with terror, although it now seeks to use them in order to give a national appearance to the war it has waged against you. Societies which are to-day tolerated have been, even in Prussia, the object of bitter persecutions. It has not been long, for instance, since the Prussian government used severe measures to suppress the society called 'Tugendverein', taking the precaution, nevertheless, to disguise it under a different title. Doctor Jahn put himself at the head of the Black Chevaliers, who were the precursors of a body of partisans known under the name of the Black Chasseurs, and commanded by Colonel Lutzow. In Prussia the still vivid memory of the late queen exercised a great influence over the new direction given to its institutions, in which she occupied the place of an occult divinity. During her lifetime she gave to Baron Nostitz a silver chain, which as her gift became the decoration, or we might rather say the rallying signal, of a new society, to which was given the name of the Conederation of Louise. And lastly, M. Lang declared himself the chief of an order of Concordists, which he instituted in imitation of the associations of that name which had for some time existed in the universities.

"My duties as magistrate," added M. Gentz, "have frequently enabled me to obtain exact information concerning these new institutions; and you may consider the information which I give you on this subject as perfectly authentic. The three chiefs whom I have just mentioned apparently direct three separate societies; but it is very certain that the three are in reality only one, since these gentlemen engage themselves to follow in every particular the vagaries of the Tugendverein, and are scattered throughout Germany in order that by their personal presence they may have a more direct influence. M. Jahn is more especially in control of Prussia; M. Lang of the north, and Baron de Nostitz of the south, of Germany. The latter, knowing perhaps the influence of a woman over young converts, associated with himself a beautiful actress named Madame Brede; and she has already been the means of making a very important acquisition to the Confederation of Louise, and one which might become still more so in the future if the French should meet with reverses. The former Elector of Hesse, admitted through the influence of Madame Brede, accepted almost immediately after his reception the grand chieftancy of the Confederation of Louise, and the very day of his installation placed in the hands of M. de Nostitz the sum necessary to create and equip a free corps of seven hundred men destined to enter the service of Prussia. It is true that having once obtained possession of this sum the baron did nothing towards the formation of the corps, which greatly incensed the ex-elector; but by dint of skill and diplomacy Madame Brede succeeded in reconciling them. It has been proved, in fact, that M, de Nostitz did not appropriate the funds deposited with him, but used them for other purposes than the arming of a free corps. M. de Nostitz is beyond doubt the most zealous, ardent, and capable of the three chiefs. I do not know him personally, but I know he is one of those men best calculated to obtain unbounded influence over all with whom he comes in contact. He succeeded in gaining such dominion over M. Stein, the Prussian minister, that the latter placed two of his secretaries at the disposal of Baron de Nostitz to prepare under his direction the pamphlets with which Germany is flooded; but I cannot too often repeat," continued M. Gentz, "that the hatred against the French avowed by these various societies is simply an accidental thing, a singular creation of circumstances; since their prime object was the overthrow of the government as it existed in Germany, and their fundamental principle the establishment of a system of absolute equality. This is so true that the question has been earnestly debated amongst the members of the Tugendverein of proclaiming the sovereignty of the people throughout Germany; and they have openly declared that the war should not be waged in the name of the governments, which according to their belief are only the instruments. I do not know what will be the final result of all these machinations; but it is very certain that by giving themselves an assumed importance these secret societies have given themselves a very real one. According to their version it is they alone who have decided the King of Prussia to openly declare himself against France, and they boast loudly that they will not stop there. After all, the result will probably be the same as in nearly all such cases,—if they are found useful they will be promised wonderful things in order to gain their allegiance, and will be abandoned when they no longer serve the intended purposes; for it is an entire impossibility that reasonable governments should lose sight of the real end for which they are instituted."

This is, I think, an exact summary, not of all M. Gentz said to me concerning the secret societies of Germany, but of what I recall; and I also remember that when I gave the Emperor an account of this conversation, his Majesty deigned to give most earnest attention, and even made me repeat certain parts, which, however, I do not now remember positively. As to the Carbonari, there is every reason to think that they belonged by secret ramifications to the German societies; but as I have already said, I have not been able to obtain exact information as to them. Nevertheless, I will endeavor to repeat here what I heard concerning the initiation of a Carbonari.

This story, which may perhaps be only imaginary, struck my attention deeply. Moreover, I give it here with much hesitation, not knowing whether some one has not already profited by it, as I was by no means the only auditor of this narration. I obtained it from a Frenchman who lived in the north of Italy at the time my conversation with M. Gentz occurred.

A French officer, formerly attached to General Moreau, a man of enthusiastic but at the same time gloomy and melancholy character, left the service after the trial instituted against his general at Paris. He took no part in the conspiracy; but unalterably attached to republican principles, this officer, whose tastes were very simple, and who possessed an ample competence, left France when the Empire was established, and took no pains to disguise his aversion to the head of an absolute government. Finally, although of most inoffensive conduct, he was one of those designated under the name of malcontents. After traveling several years in Greece, Germany, and Italy, he settled himself in a little village in the Venetian Tyrol. There he lived a very retired life, holding little communication with his neighbors, occupied in the study of natural science, given up to meditation, and no longer occupying himself, so to speak, with public affairs. This was his position, which appeared mysterious to some persons, at the time the institution of the ventes of the Carbonari were making such incredible progress in most of the Italian provinces, especially in those on the borders of the Adriatic. Several notable inhabitants of the country, who were ardent Carbonari, conceived the plan of enrolling in their society this French officer, whom they knew, and being aware of his implacable resentment against the chief of the Imperial government, whom he regarded as a great man, in fact, but at the same time as the destroyer of his beloved republic. In order not to rouse the supposed susceptibilities of this officer, they organized a hunting-party to meet in the locality where he usually took his solitary rambles. This plan was adopted, and so well carried out that the intended meeting took place apparently by chance. The officer did not hesitate to engage in conversation with the hunters, some of whom he already knew; and after some desultory remarks the conversation turned on the Carbonari, those new votaries of secret liberty. The magic word liberty had not lost its power to stir to its depths the heart of this officer, and consequently produced upon him the exact effect they desired, by awaking enthusiastic memories of his youth, and a joy to which he had long been a stranger; and consequently when they proposed to add his name to the brotherhood which was now around him, no difficulty was experienced. The officer was received, the secret signs and words of recognition were given him, and he took the oath by which he engaged to be always and at every hour at the disposal of his brethren, and to perish rather than betray their secrets; and was then initiated and continued to live as in the past, but expecting every moment a summons.

The adventurous character of the inhabitants of the Venetian Tyrol afford a striking contrast to the character of the inhabitants of Italy; but they have in common suspicious natures, and from suspicion to revenge the descent is rapid. The French officer had hardly been admitted, than there were found among them some who condemned this action, and regarded it as dangerous; and there were some who even went so far as to say that his being a Frenchman should have been a sufficient impediment, and that, besides, at a time when the police were employing their best men to uncover all disguises, it was necessary that the firmness and constancy of the newly elected should be put to some other proof than the simple formalities they had required. The sponsors of the officer, those who had, so to speak, earnestly desired him as a brother, raised no objections, being perfectly satisfied as to the correctness of their choice.

This was the state of affairs when news of the disaster of the French army at Leipzig were received in the neighboring provinces of the Adriatic, and redoubled the zeal of the Carbonari. About three months had passed since the reception of the French officer; and having received no news from his brethren, he thought that the duties of the Carbonari must be very inconsiderable, when one day he received a mysterious letter enjoining him to be the following night in a neighboring wood, at a certain spot exactly at midnight, and to wait there until some, one came to him. The officer was promptly at the rendezvous at the appointed hour, and remained until daylight, though no one appeared. He then returned to his home, thinking that this had been simply a proof of his patience. His convictions, in this respect, were somewhat changed, however, when a few days afterwards he received another letter ordering him to present himself in the same manner at the same spot; and he again passed the night there in vain expectation.

Nothing further had occurred, when a third and similar rendezvous was appointed, at which the French officer presented himself with the same punctuality and inexhaustible patience. He had waited several hours, when suddenly, instead of witnessing the arrival of his brethren, he heard the clash of swords; and moved by irresistible impulse, he rushed towards the spot from which the noise issued and seemed to recede as he advanced. He soon arrived at a spot where a frightful crime had just been committed, and saw a man weltering in his blood, attacked by two assassins. Quick as lightning he threw himself, sword in hand, on the two murderers; but, as they immediately disappeared in the thick woods, he was devoting his attention to their victim, when four gendarmes arrived on the scene; and the officer then found himself alone with unsheathed sword near the murdered man. The latter, who still breathed, made a last effort to speak, and expired while indicating his defender as his murderer, wherepon the gendarmes arrested him; and two of them took up the corpse, while the others fastened the arms of the officer with ropes, and escorted him to a neighboring village, one league distant, where they arrived at break of day. He was there conducted before a magistrate, questioned, and incarcerated in the prison of the place.

Imagine the situation of this officer, with no friends in that country, not daring to recommend himself to his own government, by whom his well- known opinions had rendered him suspected, accused of a horrible crime, well aware of all the proofs against him, and, above all, completely crushed by the last words of the dying man! Like all men of firm and resolute character, he accepted the situation without complaint, saw that it was without remedy, and resigned himself to his fate. Meanwhile, a special commission had been appointed, in order to make at least a pretense of justice; but when he was led before this commission, he could only repeat what he had already said; that is to say, give an exact account of the occurrence, protest his innocence, and admit at the same time that appearances were entirely against him. What could he reply when asked wherefore, and with what motive, he had been found alone in the night, armed with a sword, in the thickest of the wood? Here his oath as Carbonari sealed his lips, and his hesitation was taken as additional proof. What could he reply to the deposition of the gendarmes who had arrested him in the very act? He was consequently unanimously condemned to death, and reconducted to his prison until the time fixed for the execution of his sentence.

A priest was first sent to him. The officer received him with the utmost respect, but refused to make confession, and was next importuned by the visit of a brotherhood of penitents. At last the executioner came to conduct him to the place of punishment; and while he was on the way, accompanied by several gendarmes and a long line of penitents, the funeral procession was interrupted by the unexpected arrival of the colonel of the gendarmerie, whom chance brought to the scene. This officer bore the name of Colonel Boizard, a man well known in all upper Italy, and the terror of all malefactors. The colonel ordered a halt, for the purpose of himself questioning the condemned, and made him give an account of the circumstances of the crime and the sentence. When he was alone with the officer, he said, "You see that all is against you, and nothing can save you from the death which awaits you. I can, nevertheless, save you, but only on one condition. I know that you belong to the society of the Carbonari. Give me the names of your accomplices in these terrible conspiracies and your life shall be the reward."—"Never!"—"Consider, nevertheless."—"Never, I tell you; lead me to execution."

It was then necessary to set out anew for the place of execution. The executioner was at his post; and as the officer with a firm step mounted the fatal scaffold, Colonel Boizard rushed up to him and begged him still to save his life on the conditions he had offered. "No! no! never!" Instantly the scene changed; the colonel, the executioner, the gendarmes, the priest, penitents, and spectators, all gathered round the officer, each one eager to press him to their hearts, and he was conducted in triumph to his dwelling. All that had passed was simply an initiation. The assassins in the forest and their victim, as well as the judges and the pretended Colonel Boizard, had been playing a role; and the most suspicious Carbonari now knew how far their new brother would carry the constancy of his heroism and the observance of his oath.

This is almost exactly the recital which I heard, as I have said, with the deepest interest, and which I take the liberty of repeating, though I well understand how much it will lose by being written. Can it be implicitly believed? This is what I would not undertake to decide; but I can affirm that my informant gave it as the truth, and was perfectly certain that the particulars would be found in the archives of Milan, since this extraordinary initiation was at the time the subject of a circumstantial report addressed to the vice-king, whom fate had determined should nevermore see the Emperor.

CHAPTER XVIII

I digressed considerably, in the preceding chapter, from my recollections of Paris subsequent to our return from Germany after the battle of Leipzig, and the Emperor's short sojourn at Mayence. I cannot even now write the name of the latter town without recalling the spectacle of tumult and confusion which it presented after the glorious battle of Hanau, where the Bavarians fought so bravely on this the first occasion when they presented themselves as enemies before those in whose ranks they had so recently stood. It was, if I am not mistaken, in this last engagement that the Bavarian general, Wrede, was, with his family, the immediate victims of their treachery. The general, whom the Emperor had overwhelmed with kindness, was mortally wounded, all his relatives in the Bavarian army were slain, and his son-in-law, Prince of Oettingen, met the same fate. It was one of those events which never failed to make a deep impression on the mind of his Majesty, since it strengthened his ideas of fatality. It was also at Mayence that the Emperor gave orders for the assembling of the Corps Legislatif on the 2d of December. The opening was delayed, as we shall see; and far better would it have been had it been indefinitely postponed; since in that case his Majesty would not have experienced the misfortunes he afterwards endured from their opposition, symptoms of which now manifested themselves for the first time in a manner which was, to say the least, intemperate.

One of the things which astonished me most at the time, and which still astonishes me when I recall it now, was the incredible activity of the Emperor, which, far from diminishing, seemed to increase each day, as if the very exercise of his strength redoubled it. At the period of which I now speak, it is impossible to describe how completely every moment of his Majesty's time was filled. Since he had again met the Empress and his son, the Emperor had resumed his accustomed serenity; and I rarely surprised him in that open abandonment to dejection to which he sometimes gave way, in the retirement of his chamber, immediately after our return from Moscow. He was occupied more ostensibly than usual in the numerous public works which were being prosecuted in Paris, and which formed a useful distraction to his engrossing thoughts of war and the distressing news which reached him from the army. Almost every day, troops, equipped as if by magic, were reviewed by his Majesty, and ordered immediately to the Rhine, nearly the whole course of which was threatened; and the danger, which we then scarcely thought possible, must have appeared most imminent to the inhabitants of the capital, not infatuated, like ourselves, by the kind of charm the Emperor exercised over all those who had the honor of approaching his august person. In fact, for the first time he was compelled to demand of the senate to anticipate the levy for the ensuing year, and each day also brought depressing news. The prince arch-treasurer returned the following autumn, forced to quit Holland after the evacuation of this kingdom by our troops; whilst Marshal Gouvion Saint-Cyr was compelled at Dresden to sign a capitulation for himself and the thirty thousand men whom he had held in reserve at that place.

The capitulation of Marshal Saint-Cyr will never, surely, occupy an honorable place in the history of the cabinet of Vienna. It is not my province to pass judgment on these political combinations; but I cannot forget the indignation which was generally manifested at the palace when it was learned that this capitulation had been shamelessly violated by those who had now become the stronger party. It was stated in this capitulation that the marshal should return to France with the troops under his command, carrying with him a part of his artillery, and that these troops should be exchanged for a like number of the allied troops; that the wounded French who remained at Dresden should be returned to France on their restoration to health; and that, finally, the marshal should begin these movements on the 16th of November. No part of this agreement was complied with. Imagine, then, the indignation of the Emperor, already so deeply afflicted by the capitulation of Dresden, when he learned that, contrary to every stipulation agreed upon, these troops had been made prisoners by the Prince von Swarzenberg. I remember one day the Prince de Neuchatel being in his Majesty's cabinet, which I happened to enter at the moment, the Emperor remarked to him, with considerable vehemence, "You speak to me of peace. How can I believe in the good faith of those people? You see what happened at Dresden. No, I tell you, they do not wish to treat with us; they are only endeavoring to gain time, and it is our business not to lose it." The prince did not reply; or, at least, I heard no more, as I just then left the cabinet, having executed the duty which had taken me there. Moreover, I can add, as an additional proof of the confidence with which his Majesty honored me, that when I entered he never interrupted himself in what he was saying, however important it might be; and I dare to affirm that if my memory were better, these souvenirs would contain much more valuable information.

Since I have spoken of the evil tidings which overwhelmed the Emperor in such quick succession during the last months of the year 1813, there is one I should not omit, since it affected his Majesty so painfully. I refer to the death of Count Louis de Narbonne. Of all those who had not begun their careers under the eyes of the Emperor, M. de Narbonne was the one for whom he felt the deepest affection; and it must be admitted that it was impossible to find a man in whom genuine merit was united to more attractive manners. The Emperor regarded him as a most proper person to conduct a negotiation, and said of him one day, "Narbonne is a born ambassador." It was known in the palace why the Emperor had appointed him his aide-decamp at the time he formed the household of the Empress Marie Louise. The Emperor had at first intended to appoint him chevalier of honor to the new Empress, but a skillfully concocted intrigue caused him to refuse this position; and it was in some degree to make amends for this that he received the appointment of aide-de-camp to his Majesty. There was not at that time a position more highly valued in all France; many foreign and even sovereign princes had solicited in vain this high mark of favor, and amongst these I can name Prince Leopold de Saxe- Coburg,

> [Later he became King of the Belgians (in 1831), and the next year married the daughter of Louis Philippe. His first wife, Princess Charlotte of England, whom he married in 1816, died the same year. Leopold was born 1790, and died 1865.]

who married Princess Charlotte of England, and who refused to be King of Greece, after failing to obtain the position of aide-de-camp to the Emperor.

I would not dare to say, according to my recollection, that no one at the court was jealous on seeing M. de Narbonne appointed aide-de-camp to the Emperor; but if there were any I have forgotten their names. However that may have been, he soon became very popular, and each day the Emperor appreciated more highly his character and services. I remember on one occasion to have heard his Majesty say—I think it was at Dresden—that he had never thoroughly known the cabinet of Vienna until the fine nose of Narbonne—that was the Emperor's expression—had scented out those old diplomats. After the pretended negotiations, of which I have spoken above, and which occupied the entire time of the armistice at Dresden, M. de Narbonne had remained in Germany, where the Emperor had committed to him the government of Torgau; and it was there he died, on the 17th of November, in consequence of a fall from his horse, in spite of all the attentions lavished on him by Baron Desgenettes. With the exception of the death of Marshal Duroc and Prince Poniatowski, I do not remember to have ever seen the Emperor show more sincere sorrow than on this occasion. Meanwhile, almost at the very moment he lost M. de Narbonne, but before he had heard of his death, the Emperor had made arrangements to fill the place near his person of the man he had loved most, not even excepting

General Desaix. He had just called General Bertrand to the high position of grand marshal of the palace; and this choice was generally approved by all who had the honor of Count Bertrand's acquaintance. But what is there for me to say here of a man whose name in history will never be separated from that of the Emperor? This same period had seen the fall of the Duke of Istria, one of the four colonel- generals of the guard, and Marshal Duroc: and this same appointment included the names of their successors; for Marshal Suchet was appointed at the same time as General Bertrand, and took the place of Marshal Bessieres as colonel-general of the guard.

> [Louis Gabriel Suchet, born at Lyons, 1770. Served in the Italian campaign in 1796. Brigadier-general, 1797; general of division, 1799. Governor of Genoa, 1800, and served at Austerlitz, 1805. For his brilliant services in Spain he was created Duke of Albufera and marshal, 1811. At St. Helena, Napoleon stated he was the ablest of his generals then surviving. Suchet married the niece of the wives of Joseph Bonaparte and Bernadotte, and his widow died as recently as 1891. Suchet died 1826.]

At the same time his Majesty made several other changes in the higher offices of the Empire. A committee of the senate having conferred on the Emperor the right to appoint, of his own choice, the president of the Corps Legislatif, his Majesty bestowed this presidency on the Duke of Massa, who was replaced in his former position as grand judge by Count Mole, the youngest of the Emperor's ministers. The Duke of Bassano became the secretary of state, and the Duke of Vicenza received the portfolio of foreign relations.

As I have said, during the autumn of 1813 his Majesty frequently visited the public works. He usually went almost unattended, and on foot, to visit those of the Tuileries and the Louvre, and afterwards mounted his horse, accompanied by one or two officers at most, and M. Fontaine, and went to examine those which were more distant. One day,—it was about the end of November, having seized the opportunity of his Majesty's absence to take a walk through the Faubourg Saint Germain, I unexpectedly encountered his Majesty on his way to the Luxembourg, just as he arrived at the entrance of the Rue de Tournon; and it is impossible to describe the intense satisfaction with which I heard shouts of "Vive l'Empereur" break forth as he approached. I found myself driven by the crowd very near the Emperor's horse, and yet I did not imagine for a moment that he had recognized me. On his return, however, I had proofs to the contrary. His Majesty had seen me; and as I assisted him to change his clothing the Emperor gayly remarked to me, "Well, M. le Drole! Ah! ah! what were you doing in the Faubourg Saint Germain? I see just how it is! A fine thing really! You spy on me when I go out," and many other jests of the same kind; for on that day the Emperor was in such fine spirits that I concluded he had been much pleased with his visit.

Whenever at this time the Emperor experienced any unusual anxiety, I noticed that in order to dispel it he took pleasure in exhibiting himself in public more frequently, perhaps, than during his other sojourns in Paris, but always without any ostentation. He went frequently to the theater; and, thanks to the obliging kindness of Count de Remusat, I myself frequently attended these assemblies, which at that time always had the appearance of a fete. Assuredly, when on the occasion of the first representation of the ballet of Nina, their Majesties entered their box, it would have been difficult to imagine that the Emperor had already enemies among his subjects. It is true that the mothers and widows in mourning were not there; but I can affirm that I have never seen more perfect enthusiasm. The Emperor enjoyed this from the depths of his heart, even more, perhaps, than after his victories. The conviction that he was beloved by the French people impressed him deeply, and in the evening he condescended to speak to me of it—shall I dare to say like a child puffed up with pride at the reward he has just received? Then in the perfect freedom of privacy he said repeatedly, "My wife! my good Louise! Truly, she should be well satisfied." The truth is, that the desire to see the Emperor at the theater was so great in Paris, that as he always took his place in the box at the side, opening on the proscenium, each time that he made his appearance there the boxes situated on the opposite side of the hall were rented at incredible figures, and even the uppermost tiers were preferred to those from which they could not see him easily. No one who lived in Paris at that time can fail to recognize the correctness of this statement.

Some time after the first representation of the ballet of Nina, the Emperor again attended the theater, and I was also present. As formerly, the Emperor accompanied her Majesty; and I could not keep back the thought, as the play proceeded, that the Emperor had some memories sufficient to distract his attention from the exquisite music. It was at the Italian theater then occupying the Odeon. The Cleopatra of Nazzolini was played; and the representation was among the number of those called extraordinary, since it was on the occasion of Madame Grassini's benefit. It had been only a short while since this singer, celebrated in more ways than one, had first appeared in public on a Parisian stage, I think this was really only the third or fourth time; and I should state, in order to be exactly correct, that she did not produce on the Parisian public exactly the impression which had been expected from her immense reputation. It had been long since the Emperor had received her privately; but, nevertheless, her voice and Crescentini's had been reserved until then for the privileged ears of the spectators of

Saint- Cloud and the theater of the Tuileries. On, this occasion the Emperor was very generous towards the beneficiary, but no interview resulted; for, in the language of a poet of that period, the Cleopatra of Paris did not conquer another Antony.

Thus, as we see, the Emperor on a few occasions laid aside the important affairs which occupied him, less to enjoy the theater than for the purpose of showing himself in public. All useful undertakings were the objects of his care; and he did not depend entirely even on the information of men to whom he had most worthily committed them, but saw everything for himself. Among the institutions especially protected by his Majesty, there was one in which he took an especial interest. I do not think that in any of the intervals between his wars the Emperor had come to Paris without making a visit to the institution of the Daughters of the Legion of Honor, of which Madame Campan was in charge, first at Ecouen, and afterwards at Saint-Denis. The Emperor visited it in the month of November, and I remember an anecdote which I heard related to his Majesty on this occasion which diverted him exceedingly. Nevertheless, I cannot remember positively whether this anecdote relates to the visit of 1813, or one made previously.

In the first place, it must be explained that, in accordance with the regulation of the household of the young ladies of the Legion of Honor, no man, with the exception of the Emperor, was admitted into the interior of the establishment. But as the Emperor was always attended by an escort, his suite formed in some sort a part of himself, and entered with him. Besides his officers, the pages usually accompanied him. In the evening on his return from Saint-Denis, the Emperor said to me, laughing, as he entered his room, where I was waiting to undress him, "Well, my pages wish to resemble the pages of former times! The little idiots! Do you know what they do? When I go to Saint-Denis, they have a contest among themselves as to who shall be on duty. Ha! ha!" The Emperor, while speaking, laughed and rubbed his hands together; and then, having repeated several times in the same tone; "The little idiots," he added, following out one of those singular reflections which sometimes struck him, "I, Constant, would have made a very poor page; I would never have had such an idea. Moreover, these are good young men; good officers have already come from among them. This will lead one day to some marriages." It was very rare, in fact, that a thing, though frivolous in appearance, did not lead, on the Emperor's part, to some serious conclusion. Hereafter, indeed, with the exception of a few remembrances of the past, I shall have only serious and often very sad events to relate; for we have now arrived at the point where everything has taken a serious turn, and clothed itself in most somber tints.

CHAPTER XIX

For the last time we celebrated in Paris the anniversary fete of his Majesty's coronation. The gifts to the Emperor on this occasion were innumerable addresses made to him by all the towns of the Empire, in which offers of sacrifices and protestations of devotion seemed to increase in intensity in proportion to the difficulty of the circumstances. Alas! in four months the full value of these protestations was proved; and, nevertheless, how was it possible to believe that this enthusiasm, which was so universal, was not entirely sincere? This would have been an impossibility with the Emperor, who, until the very end of his reign, believed himself beloved by France with the same devotion which he felt for her. A truth, which was well proved by succeeding events, is that the Emperor became more popular among that part of the inhabitants called the people when misfortunes began to overwhelm him. His Majesty had proofs of this in a visit he made to the Faubourg Saint-Antoine; and it is very certain that, if under other circumstances he had been able to bend from his dignity to propitiate the people, a means which was most repugnant to the Emperor in consequence of his remembrances of the Revolution, all the faubourgs of Paris would have armed themselves in his defense. How can this be doubted after the event which I here describe?

The Emperor, towards the end of 1813 or the beginning of 1814, on one occasion visited the Faubourg Saint-Antoine. I cannot to-day give the precise date of this unexpected visit; but at any rate he showed himself on this occasion familiar, even to the point of good fellowship, which emboldened those immediately around to address him. I now relate the conversation which occurred between his Majesty and several of the inhabitants, which has been faithfully recorded, and admitted to be true by several witnesses of this really touching scene.

An Inhabitant.—"Is it true, as I am told, that the condition of affairs is so bad?"

The Emperor.—"I cannot say that they are in a very good condition."

The Inhabitant.—"But how, then, will all this end?"

The Emperor.—"By my faith, God alone knows."

The Inhabitant.—"But what! Is it possible the enemy could really enter France?"

The Emperor.—"That might occur, and they might even penetrate as far as this place, if you do not come to my aid. I have not a million arms. I cannot do everything alone."

Numerous Voices.—"We will uphold you, we will uphold you."

Still more Voices.—"Yes, yes. Count on us."

The Emperor.—"In that case the enemy will be beaten, and we will preserve our glory untarnished."

Several Voices.—"But what, then, shall we do?"

The Emperor.—"Be enrolled and fight."

A New Voice.—"We would do this gladly, but we would like to make certain conditions."

The Emperor.—"Well, speak out frankly. Let us know; what are these conditions?"

Several Voices.—"That we are not to pass the frontiers."

The Emperor.—"You shall not pass them."

Several Voices.—"We wish to enter the guard."

The Emperor.—"Well, then, you shall enter the guard."

His Majesty had hardly pronounced these last words, when the immense crowd which surrounded him made the air resound with cries of "Vive l'Empereur!" and their number continued to increase all the way as the Emperor slowly returned to the Tuileries, until, by the time he reached the gates of the Carrousel, he was accompanied by an innumerable cortege. We heard these noisy acclamations; but they were so badly interpreted by the commandant of the post at the palace, that he thought it was an insurrection, and the iron gates of the Tuileries on that side of the court were closed.

When I saw the Emperor, a few moments after his return, he appeared more annoyed than pleased; for everything having an appearance of disorder was excessively distasteful to him, and a popular tumult, whatever its cause, had always in it something unpleasant to him.

Meanwhile this scene, which his Majesty might well have repeated, produced a deep impression on the people; and this enthusiasm had positive and immediate results, since on that day more than two thousand men were voluntarily enrolled, and formed a new regiment of the guard.

On the anniversary fete of the coronation and of the battle of Austerlitz, there were as usual free representations in all the theaters of Paris; but at these the Emperor did not appear, as he had so often done. There were also amusements, a free distribution of eatables, and also illuminations; and twelve young girls, whose marriage dowries were given by the city of Paris, were married to old soldiers. I remember that among everything which marked the ceremonials of the Empire, the custom of performing these marriages was the one most pleasing to the Emperor, and he often spoke of it in terms of approbation; for, if I may be allowed to make the observation, his Majesty had what might be called a kind of mania on the subject of marriage. We were now settled at the Tuileries, which the Emperor had not left since the 20th of November when he had returned from Saint-Cloud, and which he did not leave again until his departure for the army. His Majesty often presided over the deliberations of the council of state, which were of grave interest. I learned at that time, in relation to a certain decree, a circumstance which appeared to me very singular. The Commune of Montmorency had long since lost its ancient name; but it was not until the end of November, 1813, that the Emperor legally took away the name of Emile which it had received under the republic in honor of J. J. Rousseau. It may well be believed that it had retained it so long simply because the Emperor's attention had not been directed to it sooner.

I do not know but I should ask pardon for relating so trivial an event, when so many great measures were being adopted by his Majesty. In fact, each day necessitated new dispositions, since the enemy was making progress at every point. The Russians occupied Holland under the command of General Witzengerode, who had opposed us so bitterly during the Russian campaign; already, even, the early return to Amsterdam of the heir of the House of Orange was discussed; in Italy Prince Eugene was holding out only by dint of superior skill against the far more numerous army of Bellegarde, who had just passed the Adige; that of the Prince von Swarzenberg occupied the confines of Switzerland; the Prussians and the troops of the Confederation were passing the Rhine at several points. There remained to the Emperor not a single ally, as the King of Denmark, the only one who had until now remained faithful, had succumbed to the northern torrent, and concluded an armistice with Russia; and in the south all the strategy of Marshal Soult barely sufficed to delay the progress of the Duke of Wellington, who was advancing on our frontiers at the head of an army far more numerous than that with which we could oppose him, and which, moreover, was not suffering from the same privations as our own. I remember well to have heard several generals blame the Emperor at that time, because he had not abandoned Spain, and recalled all his troops to France. I make a note of this, but, as may well be believed, am not willing to risk my judgment on such matters. At all events, it is evident that war surrounded us on every side; and in this state of affairs, and with our ancient frontiers threatened, it would have been strange if there had not been a general cry for peace. The Emperor desired it also; and no one now holds a contrary opinion. All the works which I have read, written by those persons best situated to learn the exact truth of these events, agree on this point. It is known that his Majesty had dictated to the Duke of Bassano a letter in which he adhered to the basis of the proposal for a new congress made at Frankfort by the allies. It is also known that the city of Mannheim was designated for the session of this new congress, to which the Duke of Vicenza was to be sent. The latter, in a note of the 2d of December, made known again the adhesion of the Emperor to the original principles and summary to be submitted to the Congress of Mannheim. The Count de Metternich, on the 10th, replied to this communication that the sovereigns would inform their allies of his Majesty's adhesion. All these negotiations were prolonged only on account of the allies, who finally declared at Frankfort that they would not consent to lay down their arms. On the 20th of December they openly announced their intention to invade France by passing through Switzerland, whose neutrality had been solemnly recognized by treaty. At the period of which I speak, my position kept me, I must admit, in complete ignorance of these affairs; but, on learning them since, they have awakened in me other remembrances which have powerfully contributed to prove their truth. Every one, I hope, will admit that if the Emperor had really desired war, it is not before me he would have taken the trouble to express his desire for the conclusion of peace, as I heard him do several times; and this by no means falsifies what I have related of a reply given by his Majesty to the Prince of Neuchatel, since in this reply he attributes the necessity of war to the bad faith of his enemies. Neither the immense renown of the Emperor nor his glory needs any support from me, and I am not deluding myself on this point; but I ask to be allowed like any other man to give my mite of the truth.

I have said previously, that when passing through Mayence the Emperor had convened the Corps Legislatif for the 2d of December; but by a new decree it was postponed until the 19th of that month, and this annual solemnity was marked by the introduction of unaccustomed usages. In the first place, as I have said, to the Emperor alone was given the right of naming the president without the presentation of a triple list, as was done in former times by the senate; moreover, the senate and the council of state repaired in a body to the hall of the Corps Legislatif to be present at the opening of the session. I also remember that this ceremony was anticipated with more than usual interest; since throughout Paris all were curious and eager to hear the address of the Emperor, and what he would say on the situation of France. Alas, we were far from supposing that this annual ceremony would be the last.

The senate and the council of state, having taken the places indicated to them in the hall, the Empress, arrived, and entered the reserved gallery, surrounded by her ladies and the officers of her household. At last the Emperor appeared, a quarter of an hour after the Empress, and was introduced with the accustomed ceremonials. When the new president, the Duke of Massa, had taken the oath at the hands of the Emperor, his Majesty pronounced the following discourse:

> "Senators; Councilors of State; Deputies from the Departments to the Corps Legislatif:
>
> Brilliant victories have made the French arms illustrious in this campaign, but unexampled defections have rendered these victories useless. Everything has turned against us. Even France would be in danger were it not for the energy and union of the French people.
>
> Under these momentous circumstances my first thought was to summon you. My heart felt the need of the presence and affection of my subjects.
>
> I have never been seduced by prosperity; adversity will find me above the reach of its attacks. I have many times given peace to nations, even when they had lost all. On a part of my conquests I have erected thrones for kings who have now abandoned me.
>
> I have conceived and executed great plans for the happiness of the world. Both as a monarch and a father I feel that peace adds to the security of thrones and of families. Negotiations have been entered into with the Confederated Powers. I have adhered to the fundamental principles which they have presented. I then hoped that, before the opening of this session, the Congress of Mannheim would have assembled; but renewed delays, which cannot be attributed to France, have deferred this moment, which the whole world so eagerly desires.
>
> I have ordered that all the original articles contained in the portfolio of Foreign Affairs should be submitted to you. You will be informed of them through a committee. The spokesmen of my Council will inform you of my wishes on this subject.
>
> Nothing has been interposed on my part to the re-establishment of peace; I know and share the sentiments

of the French people. I repeat, of the French people, since there are none among them who desire peace at the expense of honor. It is with regret that I demand of this generous people new sacrifices, but they are necessary for their noblest and dearest interests. I have been compelled to re-enforce my armies by numerous levies, for nations treat with security only when they display all their strength. An increase of receipts has become indispensable. The propositions which my minister of finance will submit to you are in conformity with the system of finance I have established. We will meet all demands without borrowing, which uses up the resources of the future, and without paper money, which is the greatest enemy of social order.

I am well satisfied with the sentiments manifested towards me under these circumstances by my people of Italy.

Denmark, and Naples alone remain faithful to their alliance. The Republic of the United States of America successfully continues its war with England. I have recognized the neutrality of the nineteen Swiss cantons.

Senators; Councillors of State; Deputies of the Departments in the Corps Legislatif:

You are the natural organs of the throne. It is your province to display an energy which will hold our country up to the admiration of all future generations. Let it not be said of us: 'They sacrificed the first interests of their country; they submitted to the control which England has sought in vain for four centuries to impose on France.'

"My people need not fear that the policy of their Emperor will ever betray the glory of the nation; and on my part I have the conviction that the French people will ever prove worthy of themselves and of me."

This address was received with unanimous shouts of "Vive l'Empereur;" and, when his Majesty returned to the. Tuileries, he had an air of intense satisfaction, although he had a slight headache, which disappeared after half an hour's repose. In the evening it was entirely gone, and the Emperor questioned me on what I had heard people say. I told, him truthfully that the persons of my acquaintance unanimously agreed that the desire for peace was universal. "Peace, peace!" said the Emperor, "who can desire it more than I? Go, my son, go." I withdrew, and his Majesty went to the Empress.

It was about this time, I do not remember the exact day, that the Emperor gave a decision on a matter in which I had interested myself with him; and I affirm that it will be seen from this decision what a profound respect his Majesty had for the rights of a legitimate marriage, and his excessive antipathy to divorced persons. But, in order to support this assertion, I will give an anecdote which recurs to my memory at this moment.

During the Russian campaign General Dupont-Derval was slain on the battlefield, fighting valiantly. His widow, after his Majesty's return to Paris, had often, but always in vain, endeavored to present a petition to his Majesty describing her unfortunate condition. At length some one advised her to secure my services; and, touched by her unhappiness, I presented her demand to the Emperor. His Majesty but rarely refused my solicitations of this kind, as I conducted them with the utmost discretion; and consequently I was fortunate enough to obtain for Madame Dupont-Derval a very considerable pension. I do not remember how the Emperor discovered that General Dupont-Derval had been divorced, and had left a daughter by a former marriage, who, as well as her mother, was still living. He learned besides that General Dupont-Derval's second wife was the widow of a general officer by whom she had two daughters. None of these circumstances, as may be imagined, had been cited in the petition; but, when they came to the Emperor's knowledge, he did not withdraw the pension, for which the order had not yet been given, but simply changed its destination, and gave it to the first wife of—General Dupont-Derval, making it revertible to her daughter, though she was sufficiently wealthy not to need it, and the other Madame Dupont-Derval was in actual need. Meanwhile, as one is always pleased to be the bearer of good tidings, I had lost no time in informing my petitioner of the Emperor's favorable decision. When she learned what had taken place, of which I was still in entire ignorance, she returned to me, and from what she said I imagined she was the victim of some mistake. In this belief I took the liberty of again speaking to his Majesty on the subject, and my astonishment may be imagined when his Majesty himself condescended to relate to me the whole affair. Then he added: "My poor child, you have allowed yourself to be taken for a simpleton. I promised a pension, and I gave it to the wife of General Derval, that is to say, to his real wife, the mother of his daughter." The Emperor was not at all angry with me. I know very well that the matter would not have been permitted to continue thus without my interesting myself further in it; but events followed each other in rapid succession until the abdication of his Majesty, and the affair finally remained as thus settled.

CHAPTER XX

It was not only by force of arms that the enemies of France endeavored at the end of 1813 to overthrow the power of the Emperor. In spite of our defeats the Emperor's name still inspired a salutary terror; and it was apparent that although so numerous, the foreigners still despaired of victory as long as there existed a common accord between the Emperor and the French people. We have seen in the preceding chapter in what language he expressed himself to the great united bodies of the state, and events have proved whether his Majesty concealed the truth from the representatives of the nation as to the real condition of France. To this discourse which history has recorded, I may be allowed to oppose here another made at the same period. This is the famous declaration of Frankfort, copies of which the enemies of the Emperor caused to be circulated in Paris; and I would not dare to wager that persons of his court, while performing their duties near him, did not have a copy in their pockets. If there still remains any doubt as to which party was acting in good faith, the reading of what follows is sufficient to dispel these; for there is no question here of political considerations, but simply the comparison of solemn promises with the actions which succeeded.

> "The French government has just ordered a new levy of three hundred thousand men; the proclamations of the senate contain a challenge to the allied powers. They find themselves called on again to promulgate to the world the views by which they are guided in this present war, the principles which form the basis of their conduct, their wishes, and their intentions. The allied powers are not making war on France, but on the openly admitted preponderance which, to the great misfortune of Europe and France, the Emperor Napoleon has too long maintained outside the limits of his Empire.
>
> Victory has brought the allied armies to the Rhine. The first use their imperial and royal Majesties have made of victory has been to offer peace to his Majesty the Emperor of the French. A position reenforced by the accession of all the sovereigns and princes of Germany has had

no influence on the conditions of this peace, for these conditions are founded on the independence of the other states of Europe. The objects of these powers are just in their aims, generous and liberal in their application, reassuring to all, and honorable to each.

The allied sovereigns desire that France should be great, strong, and happy, since its greatness and power is one of the foundations of the social edifice. They desire that France should be happy, that French commerce should revive, that the arts, those blessings of peace, should flourish, because a great people are tranquil only when satisfied. The powers confirm the French Empire in the possession of an extent of territory which France has never attained under her kings, since a generous nation should not be punished because it has experienced reverses in a bloody and well-contested struggle in which it has fought with its accustomed bravery.

But the powers themselves also wish to be happy and peaceful. They desire a condition of peace which, by a wise partition of force, by a just equilibrium, may hereafter preserve their people from the innumerable calamities which have for twenty years overwhelmed Europe.

"The allied powers will not lay down their arms until they have obtained this grand and beneficent result, the worthy object of all their efforts. They will not lay down their arms until the political condition of Europe is again secure; until immutable principles have regained their ascendency over new pretensions, and the sanctity of treaties has finally assured a genuine peace to Europe."

It needs only common sense to ascertain whether the allied powers were sincere in this declaration, the object of which evidently was to alienate from the Emperor the affections of his people by holding up his Majesty before them as an obstacle to peace, and separating his cause from that of France; and on this point I am glad to support my own opinion by that of M. de Bourrienne, whom surely no one will accuse of partiality for his Majesty.

Several passages of his Memoirs, above all those in which he blames the Emperor, have pained me, I must confess; but on this occasion he does not hesitate to admit the insincerity of the allies, which opinion is of much weight according to my poor judgment.

M. de Bourrienne was then at Paris under the special surveillance of the Duke of Rovigo. I frequently heard this minister mention him to the Emperor, and always favorably; but the enemies of the former secretary of the First Consul must have been very powerful, or his Majesty's prejudices very strong, for M. de Bourrienne never returned to favor. The Emperor, who, as I have said, sometimes condescended to converse familiarly with me, never spoke to me of M. de Bourrienne, whom I had not seen since the Emperor had ceased to receive him. I saw him again for the first time among the officers of the National Guard, the day these gentlemen were received at the palace, as we shall see later, and I have never seen him since; but as we were all much attached to him on account of his kind consideration for us, he was often the subject of conversation, and, I may add, of our regrets. Moreover, I was long ignorant that at the period of which I am now speaking, his Majesty had offered him the mission to Switzerland, as I learned this circumstance only from reading his Memoirs. I would not conceal, however, that I was painfully affected by reading this, so greatly would I have desired that Bourrienne should overcome his resentment against his Majesty, who in the depths of his heart really loved him.

Whatever was done, it is evident now to all that the object of the declaration of Frankfort was to cause alienation between the Emperor and the French people, and subsequent events have shown that this was fully understood by the Emperor, but unfortunately it was soon seen that the enemy had partly obtained their object. Not only in private society persons could be heard expressing themselves freely in condemnation of the Emperor, but dissensions openly arose even in the body of the Corps Legislatif.

After the opening session, the Emperor having rendered a decree that a commission should be named composed of five senators and five members of the Corps Legislatif, these two bodies consequently assembled. This commission, as has been seen from his Majesty's address, had for its object the consideration of articles submitted relative to pending negotiations between France and the allied powers. Count Regnault de Saint Jean d'Angely bore the decree to the Corps Legislatif, and supported it with his usual persuasive eloquence, recalling the victories of France and the glory of the Emperor; but the ballot elected as members of the commission five deputies who had the reputation of being more devoted to the principles of liberty than to the Emperor. These were M. Raynouard, Laine, Gallois, Flaugergues, and Maine de Biran. The Emperor from the first moment appeared much dissatisfied with this selection, not imagining, however, that this commission would soon show itself so entirely hostile. I remember well that I heard his Majesty say in my presence to the Prince of Neuchatel, with some exasperation though without anger, "They have appointed five lawyers."

Nevertheless, the Emperor did not allow the least symptoms of his dissatisfaction to be seen; and as soon as he had officially received the list of commissioners, addressed to the President of the Corps Legislatif the following letter bearing the date of the 23d of December:

> "MONSIEUR, Duke of Massa, President of the Legislative Corps: We address you the inclosed letter to make known to you our intention that you report to-morrow, the 24th instant, at the residence of our cousin the prince archchancellor of the Empire, in company with the commission appointed yesterday by the Legislative Corps in compliance with our decree of the 20th instant, and which is composed of the following gentlemen: Raynouard, Lain, Galiois, Flaugergues, and Maine de Biran, for the purpose of considering the articles relative to the negotiations, and also the declaration of the confederated powers, which will be communicated by Count Regnault minister of state, and Count d'Hauterive councilor of state attached to the department of foreign relations, who will be the bearer of the aforesaid articles and declaration.
>
> "Our intention also is that our cousin aforesaid should preside over this commission. With this etc."
>
> The members of the senate appointed on this commission were M. deFontanel, M. the Prince of Benevent, M. de Saint Marsan, M. de Barbe- Marbois, and M. de Beurnonville.

With the exception of one of these gentlemen, whose disgrace and consequent opposition were publicly known, the others were thought to be sincerely attached to the Emperor; and whatever may have been their opinions and their subsequent conduct they had done nothing then to deserve the same distrust from the Emperor as the members of the committee from the Corps Legislatif. No active opposition, no signs of discontent, had been shown by the conservative senate.

At this time the Duke of Rovigo came frequently, or I might rather say every day, to the Emperor. His Majesty was much attached to him, and that alone suffices to prove that he was not afraid to hear the truth; for since he had been minister, the Duke of Rovigo had never concealed it; which fact I can affirm, having been frequently an eyewitness. In Paris there was nevertheless only unanimous opposition to this minister. I can, however, cite one anecdote that the Duke of Rovigo has not included in his Memoirs, and of which I guarantee the authenticity; and it will be seen from this incident whether or not the minister of police sought to increase the number of persons who compromised themselves each day by their gratings against the Emperor.

Among the employees of the treasury was a former receiver of the finances who led a retired and contented life in this modest employment. He was a very enthusiastic man of much intelligence. His devotion to the Emperor amounted to a passion, and he never mentioned him without a sort of idolatry. This employee was accustomed to pass his evenings with a circle of friends who met in the Rue de Vivienne. The regular attendants of this place, whom the police very naturally had their eyes upon, did not all hold the same opinion as the person of whom I have just spoken, and began openly to condemn the acts of government, the opposing party allowing their discontent to be plainly manifest; and the faithful adorer of his Majesty became proportionately more lavish of his expressions of admiration, as his antagonists showed themselves ready with reproaches. The Duke of Rovigo was informed of these discussions, which each day became more eager and animated; and one fine day our honest employee found on returning to his home a letter bearing the seal of the general of police. He could not believe his eyes. He, a good, simple, modest man living his retired life, what could the minister of general police desire of him? He opens the letter, and finds that the minister orders him to appear before him the next morning. He reports there as may be imagined with the utmost punctuality, and then a dialogue something like this ensued between these gentlemen. "It appears, Monsieur," said the Duke of Rovigo, "that you are very devoted to the Emperor."—"Yes, I love him; I would give him my blood, my life."—"You admire him greatly?"— "Yes, I admire him! The Emperor has never been so great, his glory has never—"—"That is all very well, Monsieur; your sentiments do you honor, and I share those sentiments with you; but I urge on you to reserve the expression of them for yourself, for, though I should regret it very much, you may drive me to the necessity of having you arrested."—"I, my Lord, have me arrested? Ah! but doubtless—why?"—"Do you not see that you cause the expression of opinions that might remain concealed were it not for your enthusiasm; and finally, you will force, many good men to compromise themselves to a certain extent, who will return to us when things are in better condition. Go, Monsieur, let us continue to love, serve, and admire the Emperor; but at such a time as this let us not proclaim our fine sentiments so loudly, for fear of rendering many guilty who are only a little misguided." The employee of the treasury then left the minister, after thanking him for his advice and promising to follow it. I would not dare to assert that he kept his word scrupulously, but I can affirm that all I have just said is the exact truth; and I am sure that if this passage in my Memoirs falls under the eyes of the Duke of Rovigo it will remind him of an occurrence which he may perhaps have forgotten, but which he will readily recall.

Meanwhile the commission, composed as I have said of five senators and five members of the Corps Legislatif, devoted itself assiduously to the duty with which it was charged. Each of these two grand bodies of the state presented to his Majesty a separate address. The senate had received the report made by M. de Fontanes; and their address contained nothing which could displease the Emperor, but was on the contrary expressed in most proper terms. In it a peace was indeed demanded, but a peace which his Majesty could obtain by an effort worthy of him and of the French people. "Let that hand so many times victorious," they said, "lay down its arms after having assured the repose of the world." The following passage was also noteworthy: "No, the enemy shall not destroy this beautiful and noble France, which for fourteen hundred years has borne itself gloriously through such diverse fortunes, and which for the interest of the neighboring nations themselves should always bear considerable weight in the balance of power in Europe. We have as pledges of this your heroic constancy and the national honor." Then again, "Fortune does not long fail nations which do not fail in their duty to themselves."

This language, worthy of true Frenchmen, and which the circumstances at least required, was well pleasing to the Emperor, as is evident from the answer he made on the 29th of December to the deputation from the senate with the prince archchancellor at its head:

"Senators," said his Majesty, "I am deeply sensible of the sentiments you express. You have seen by the articles which I have communicated to you what I am doing towards a peace. The sacrifices required by the preliminary basis which the enemy had proposed to me I have accepted; and I shall make them without regret, since my life has only one object,—the happiness of the French people.

"Meanwhile Bearn, Alsace, Franche-Comte, and Brabant have been entered, and the cries of that part of my family rend my soul. I call the French to the aid of the French! I call the Frenchmen of Paris, Brittany, Normandy, Champagne, Burgundy, and the other departments to the aid of their brothers. Will they abandon them in misfortune? Peace and the deliverance of our territory should be our rallying cry. At the sight of this whole people in arms the foreigner will flee, or will consent to peace on the terms I have proposed to him. The question is no longer the recovery of the conquests we have made."

It was necessary to be in a position to thoroughly know the character of the Emperor to understand how much it must have cost him to utter these last words; but from a knowledge of his character also resulted the certainty that it would have cost him less to do what he promised than to say them. It would seem that this was well understood in Paris; for the day on which the 'Moniteur' published the reply of his Majesty to the senate, stocks increased in value more than two francs, which the Emperor did not fail to remark with much satisfaction; for as is well known, the rise and decline of stocks was with him the real thermometer of public opinion.

In regard to the conduct of the Corps Legislatif, I heard it condemned by a man of real merit deeply imbued with republican principles. He uttered one day in my presence these words which struck me: "The Corps Legislatif did then what it should have done at all times, except under these circumstances." From the language used by the spokesman of the commission, it is only too evident that the speaker believed in the false promises of the declaration of Frankfort. According to him, or rather according to the commission of which he was after all only the organ, the intention of the foreigners was not to humiliate France; they only wished to keep us within our proper limits, and annul the effects of an ambitious activity which had been so fatal for twenty years to all the nations of Europe. "The propositions of the confederated powers," said the commission, "seem to us honorable for the nation, since they prove that foreigners both fear and respect us." Finally the speaker, continuing his reading, having reached a passage in which allusion was made to the Empire of the Lily, added in set phrase that the Rhine, the Alps, the Pyrenees, and the two seas inclosed a vast territory, several provinces of which had not belonged to ancient France, and that nevertheless the crown royal of France shone brilliantly with glory and majesty among all other diadems.

At these words the Duke of Massa interrupted the speaker, exclaiming, "What you say is unconstitutional;" to which the speaker vehemently replied, "I see nothing unconstitutional here except your presence," and continued to read his report. The Emperor was each day informed of what took place in the sitting of the Corps Legislatif; and I remember that the day on which their report was read he, appeared much disturbed, and before retiring walked up and down the room in much agitation, like one trying to make some important decision. At last he decided not to allow the publication of the address of the Corps Legislatif, which had been communicated to him according to custom. Time pressed; the next day would have been too late, as the address would be circulated in Paris, where the public mind was already much disturbed. The order was consequently given to the minister of general police to have the copy of the report and the address seized at the printing establishment, and to break the forms already set up. Besides this the order was also given to close the doors of the Corps Legislatif, which was done, and the legislature thus found itself adjourned.

I heard many persons at this time deeply regret that his Majesty had taken these measures, and, above all, that having taken them he had not stopped there. It was said that since the Corps Legislatif was now adjourned by force, it was better, whatever might be the result, to convoke another chamber, and that the Emperor should not recognize the members of the one he had dismissed. His Majesty thought otherwise, and gave the deputies a farewell audience. They came to the Tuileries; and there his only too just resentment found vent in these words:

"I have suppressed your address, as it was incendiary. Eleven-twelfths of the Corps Legislatif are composed of good citizens whom I know and for whom I have much regard; the other twelfth is composed of seditious persons who are devoted to England. Your Commission and its chairman, M. Laine, are of this number. He corresponds with the Prince Regent, through the lawyer Deseze. I know it, and have proof of it. The other four are of the same faction. If there are abuses to be remedied, is this a time for remonstrances, when two hundred thousand Cossacks are crossing our frontiers? Is this the moment to dispute as to individual liberty and safety, when the question is the preservation of political liberty and national independence? The enemy must be resisted; you must follow the example of the Alsatians, Vosges, and inhabitants of Franche- Comte, who wish to march against them, and have applied to me-for arms. You endeavor in your address to separate the sovereign from the nation. It is I who here represent the people, who have given me four million of their suffrages. If I believed you I should cede to the enemy more than he demands. You shall have peace in three months or I shall perish. Your address was an insult to me and to the Corps Legislatif."

Although the journals were forbidden to repeat the details of this scene, the rumors of it spread through Paris with the rapidity of lightning. The Emperor's words were repeated and commented on; the dismissed deputies sounded them through all the departments. I remember seeing the prime arch-chancellor next day come to the Emperor and request an audience; it was in favor of M. Deseze, whose protector he then was. In spite of the threatening words of his Majesty, he found him not disposed to take severe measures; for his anger had already exhausted itself, as was always the case with the Emperor when he had abandoned himself to his first emotions of fury. However, the fatal misunderstanding between the Corps Legislatif and the Emperor, caused by the report of the committee of that body, produced the most grievous effects; and it is easy to conceive how much the enemy must have rejoiced over this, as they never failed to be promptly informed by the numerous agents whom they employed in France. It was under these sad circumstances that the year 1813 closed. We will see in future what were the consequences of it, and in fact the history, until now unwritten, of the Emperor's inner life at Fontainebleau; that is to say, of the most painful period of my life.

CHAPTER, XXI

In order to neutralize the effects which might be produced in the provinces by the reports of the members of the Corps Legislatif and the correspondence of the alarmists, his Majesty appointed from the members of the conservative senate a certain number of commissioners whom he charged to visit the departments and restore public confidence. This was a most salutary measure, and one which circumstances imperiously demanded; for discouragement began to be felt among the masses of the population, and as is well known in such cases the presence of superior authority restores confidence to those who are only timid. Nevertheless, the enemy were advancing at several points, and had already pressed the soil of Old France. When this news reached the Emperor, it afflicted him deeply without overcoming him. At times, however, his indignation broke forth; above all, when he learned from the reports that French emigrants had entered the enemy's ranks, whom he stigmatized by the name of traitors, infamous and wretched creatures, unworthy of pity. I remember that on the occasion of the capture of Huningen he thus characterized a certain M. de Montjoie, who was now serving in the Bavarian army after taking a German name, which I have forgotten. The Emperor added, however: "At least, he has had the modesty not to keep his French name." In general easy to conciliate on nearly all points, the Emperor was pitiless towards all those who bore arms against their country; and innumerable times I have heard him say that there was no greater crime in his eyes.

In order not to add to the complication of so many conflicting interests which encountered and ran contrary to each other still more each day, the Emperor already had the thought of sending Ferdinand VII. back into Spain. I have the certainty that his Majesty had even made some overtures to him on this subject during his last stay in Paris; but it was the Spanish prince who objected to this, not ceasing, on the contrary, to demand the Emperor's protection. He desired most of all to become the ally, of his Majesty, and it was well known that in his letters to his Majesty he urged him incessantly to give him a wife of the Emperor's selection. The Emperor had seriously thought of marrying him to the eldest daughter of King Joseph, which seemed a means of conciliating at the same time the rights of Prince Joseph and those of Ferdinand VII., and King Joseph asked nothing better than to be made a party to this arrangement; and from the manner in which he had used his royalty since the commencement of his reign, we may be permitted to think that his Majesty did not greatly object to this. Prince Ferdinand had acquiesced in this alliance, which appeared very agreeable to him, when suddenly at the end of the year 1813 he demanded time; and the course of events placed this affair among the number of those which existed only in intention. Prince Ferdinand left Valencay at last, but later than the Emperor had authorized him to do, and for some time his presence had been only an additional embarrassment. However, the Emperor had no reason to complain of his conduct towards him until after the events of Fontainebleau.

At any rate, in the serious situation of affairs, matters concerning the Prince of Spain were only an incidental matter, no more important than the stay of the Pope at Fontainebleau; the great point, the object which predominated everything, was the defense of the soil of France, which the first days of January found invaded at many points. This was the one thought of his Majesty, which did not prevent him, nevertheless, from entering according to custom into all the duties of his administration; and we will soon see the measures he took to re-establish the national guard of Paris. I have on this subject certain documents and particulars which are little known, from a person whose name I am not permitted to give, but whose position gave him the opportunity of learning all the intricacies of its formation. As all these duties still required for more than a month the presence of his Majesty at Paris, he remained there until the 25th of January.

But what fatal news he received during those twenty-five days!

First the Emperor learned that the Russians, as unscrupulous as the Austrians in observing the conditions of a capitulation which are usually considered sacred, had just trampled under their feet the stipulations made at Dantzic. In the name of the Emperor Alexander, the Prince of Wurtemberg who commanded the siege had acknowledged and guaranteed to General Rapp and the troops placed under his command the right to return to France, which agreement was no more respected than had been a few months before that made with Marshal Saint-Cyr by the Prince of Schwarzenberg; thus the garrison of Dantzic were made prisoners with the same bad faith as that of Dresden had been. This news, which reached him at almost the same time as that of the surrender of Torgau, distressed his Majesty so much the more as it contributed to prove to him that these powerful enemies wished to treat of peace only in name, with a resolution to retire always before a definite conclusion was reached.

At the same period the news from Lyons was in no wise reassuring. The command of this place had been confided to Marshal Augereau, and he was accused of having lacked the energy necessary to foresee or arrest the invasion of the south of France. Further I will not now dwell on this circumstance, proposing in the following chapter to collect my souvenirs which relate more especially to the beginning of the campaign in France, and some circumstances which preceded it. I limit myself consequently to recalling, as far as my memory serves, events which occurred during the last days the Emperor passed in Paris.

From the 4th of January his Majesty, although having lost, as I said a while since, all hope of inducing the invaders to conclude a peace, which the whole world so much needed, gave his instructions to the Duke of Vicenza, and sent him to the headquarters of the allies; but he was compelled to wait a long time for his passports. At the same time special orders were sent to the prefects of departments in the invaded territory as to the conduct they should pursue under such difficult circumstances. Thinking at the same time that it was indispensable to make an example in order to strengthen the courage of the timid, the Emperor ordered the creation of a commission of inquiry, charged to inquire into the conduct of Baron Capelle, prefect of the department of the Leman at the time of the entrance of the enemy into Geneva. Finally a decree mobilized one hundred and twenty battalions of the National Guard of the Empire, and ordered a levy en masse on all the departments of the east of all men capable of bearing arms. Excellent measures doubtless, but vain! Destiny was stronger than even the genius of a great man.

Meanwhile on the 8th of January appeared the decree which called out for active duty thirty thousand men of the National Guard of Paris on the very day when by a singular and fatal coincidence the King of Naples signed a treaty of alliance with Great Britain. The Emperor reserved for himself the chief command of the National Parisian Guard, and constituted the staff as follows: a vice-commander-in-chief, four aides who were major-generals, four adjutant commandants, and eight assistant captains. A legion was formed in each district, and each legion was divided into four battalions subdivided into five companies.—Next the Emperor appointed the following to superior grades:

General vice-commander-in-chief.—Marshal de Moncey, Duke of Conegliano.

Aides—major-generals.—General of division, Count Hullin; Count Bertrand, grand marshal of the palace; Count of Montesquieu, grand chamberlain; Count de Montmorency, chamberlain of the Emperor.

Adjutant-commandants.—Baron Laborde, adjutant-commandant of the post of Paris; Count Albert de Brancas, chamberlain of the Emperor; Count Germain, chamberlain of the Emperor; M. Tourton.

Assistant captains.—Count Lariboisiere; Chevalier Adolphe de Maussion; Messieurs Jules de Montbreton, son of the equerry of the Princess Borghese; Collin, junior, the younger; Lecordier, junior; Lemoine, junior; Cardon, junior; Malet, junior.

Chiefs of the twelve Legions.—First legion, Count de Gontaut, senior; second legion, Count Regnault de Saint Jean d'Angely; third legion, Baron Hottinguer, banker; fourth legion, Count Jaubert, governor of the bank of France; fifth legion, M. Dauberjon de Murinais; sixth legion, M. de Fraguier; seventh legion, M. Lepileur de Brevannes; eighth legion, M. Richard Lenoir; ninth legion, M. Devins de Gaville; tenth legion, the Duke of Cadore; eleventh legion, Count de Choiseul-Praslin, chamberlain of the Emperor; twelfth legion, M. Salleron.

From the names we have just read, we may judge of the incredible insight by which his Majesty was enabled to choose, among the most distinguished persons of the different classes of society, those most popular and most influential from their positions. By the side of the names which had gained glory under the eyes of the Emperor, and by seconding him in his great undertakings, could be found those whose claim to distinction was more ancient and recalled noble memories, and finally the heads of the principal industries in the capital. This species of amalgamation delighted the Emperor greatly; and he must have attached to it great political importance, for this idea occupied his attention to such an extent that I have often heard him say, "I wish to confound all classes, all periods, all glories. I desire that no title may be more glorious than the title of Frenchman." Why is it fate decreed that the Emperor should not be allowed time to carry out his extensive plans for the glory and happiness of France of which he so often spoke? The staff of the National Guard and the chiefs of the twelve legions being appointed, the Emperor left the nomination of the other officers, as well as the formation of the legions, to the selection of M. de Chabrol, prefect of the Seine. This worthy magistrate, to whom the Emperor was much attached, displayed under these circumstances the greatest zeal and activity, and in a short time the National Guard presented an imposing appearance. They were armed, equipped, and clothed in the best possible manner; and this ardor, which might be called general, was in these last days one of the consolations which most deeply touched the heart of the Emperor, since he saw in it a proof of the attachment of the Parisians to his person, and an additional motive for feeling secure as to the tranquillity of the capital during his approaching absence. Be that as it may, the bureau of the National Guard was soon formed, and established in the residence which Marshal Moncey inhabited on the Rue du Faubourg Saint-Honore, near the square Beauveau; and one master of requests and two auditors of the council of state were attached to it. The master of requests, a superior officer of engineers, the Chevalier Allent, soon be came the soul of the whole administration of the National Guard, no one being more capable than he of giving a lively impulse to an organization which required great promptness. The person from whom I obtained this information, which I intermingle with my personal souvenirs, has assured me that following upon, that is to say, after our departure for Chalons- sur-Marne, M. Allent became still more influential in the National Guard, of which he was the real head. In fact, when King Joseph had received the title of lieutenant-general to the Emperor, which his Majesty conferred on him during the time of his absence, M. Allent found himself attached on one hand to the staff of King Joseph as officer of engineers, and on the other to the vice-general-in-chief in his quality of master of requests. It resulted that he was the mediator and counselor in all communications which were necessarily established between the lieutenant- general of the Emperor and Marshal Moncey, and the promptness of his decisions was a source of great benefit to that good and grave marshal. He signed all letters, "The Marshal, Duke de Conegliano;" and wrote so slowly that M. Allent had, so to speak, time to write the correspondence while the marshal was signing his name. The auditors to the council of state duties of the two were nothing, or nearly so; but these men were by no means nobodies, as has been asserted, though a few of that character of course slipped into the council, since the first condition for holding this office was simply to prove an income of at least six thousand francs. These were Messieurs Ducancel, the dean of the auditors, and M. Robert de Sainte-Croix. A shell had broken the latter's leg during the return from Moscow; and this brave young man, a captain of cavalry, had returned, seated astride a cannon, from the banks of the Beresina to Wilna. Having little physical strength, but gifted with a strong mind, M. Robert de Sainte-Croix owed it to his moral courage not to succumb; and after undergoing the amputation of his leg, left the sword for the pen, and it was thus he became auditor to the council of state.

The week after the National Guard of the city of Paris had been called into service, the chiefs of the twelve legions and the general staff were admitted to take the oath of fidelity at the Emperor's hands. The National Guard had already been organized into legions; but the want of arms was keenly felt, and many citizens could procure only lances, and those who could not obtain guns or buy them found themselves thereby chilled in their ardor to equip themselves. Nevertheless, the Citizen Guard soon enrolled the desired number of thirty thousand men, and by degrees it occupied the different posts of the capital; and whilst fathers of families and citizens employed in domestic work were enrolled without difficulty, those who had already paid their debts to their country on the battlefield also demanded to be allowed to serve her again, and to shed for her the last drop of their blood. Invalided soldiers begged to resume their service. Hundreds of these brave soldiers forgot their sufferings, and covered with honorable wounds went forth again to confront the enemy. Alas! very few of those who then left the Hotel des Invalides were fortunate enough to return.

Meanwhile the moment of the Emperor's departure approached; but before setting out he bade a touching adieu to the National Guard, as we shall see in the next chapter, and confided the regency to the Empress as he had formerly intrusted it to her during the campaign in Dresden. Alas this time it was not necessary to make a long journey before the Emperor was at the head of his army.

CHAPTER XXII

We are now about to begin the campaign of miracles; but before relating the events which I witnessed on this campaign, during which I, so to speak, never left the Emperor, it is necessary that I here inscribe some souvenirs which may be considered as a necessary introduction. It is well known that the Swiss cantons had solemnly declared to the Emperor that they would not allow their territory to be violated, and that they would do everything possible to oppose the passage of the allied armies who were marching on the frontiers of France by way of the Breisgau. The Emperor, in order to stop them on their march, relied upon the destruction of the bridge of Bale; but this bridge was not destroyed, and Switzerland, instead of maintaining her promised neutrality, entered into the coalition against France. The foreign armies passed the Rhine at Bale, at Schaffhausen, and at Mannheim. Capitulations made with the generals of the confederated troops in regard to the French garrisons of Dantzic, Dresden, and other strong towns had been, as we have seen, openly violated. Thus Marshal Gouvion Saint-Cyr and his army corps had been, contrary to the stipulations contained in the treaties, surrounded by superior forces, disarmed, and conducted as prisoners to Austria; and twenty thousand men, the remains of the garrison of Dantzic, were thus arrested by order of the Emperor Alexander, and conveyed to the Russian deserts. Geneva opened its gates to the enemy in the following January. Vesoul, Epinal, Nancy, Langres, Dijon, Chalons-sur-Saone, and Bar-sur- Aube were occupied by the allies.

The Emperor, in proportion as the danger became more pressing, displayed still more his energy and indefatigable activity. He urged the organization of new levies, and in order to pay the most urgent expenses drew thirty millions from his secret treasury in the vaults of the pavilion Marsan. The levies of conscripts were, however, made with difficulty; for in the course of the year 1813 alone, one million forty thousand soldiers had been summoned to the field, and France could no longer sustain such enormous drains. Meanwhile veterans came from all parts to be enrolled; and General Carnot offered his services to the Emperor, who was much touched by this proceeding, and confided to him the defense of Antwerp. The zeal and courage with which the general acquitted himself of this important mission is well known. Movable columns and corps of partisans placed themselves under arms in the departments of the east, and a few rich proprietors levied and organized companies of volunteers, while select cavalry formed themselves into corps, the cavaliers of which equipped themselves at their own expense.

In the midst of these preparations the Emperor received news which moved him deeply,—the King of Naples had just joined the enemies of the French. On a previous occasion, when his Majesty had seen the Prince Royal of Sweden, after having been marshal and prince of the Empire, enter into a coalition against his native country, I heard him break forth into reproaches and exclamations of indignation, although the King of Sweden had more than one reason to offer in his own defense, being alone in the north, and shut in by powerful enemies against whom he was entirely unable to struggle, even had the interests of his new country been inseparable from those of France. By refusing to enter into the coalition he would have drawn on Sweden the anger of her formidable neighbors, and with the throne he would have sacrificed and fruitlessly ruined the nation which had adopted him. It was not to the Emperor he owed his elevation. But King Joachim, on the contrary, owed everything to the Emperor; for it was he who had given him one of his sisters as a wife, who had given him a throne, and had treated him as well as, and even better than, if he had been a brother. It was consequently the duty of the King of Naples as well as his interest not to separate his cause from that of France; for if the Emperor fell, how could the kings of his own family, whom he had made, hope to stand? Both King Joseph and Jerome had well understood this, and also the brave and loyal Prince Eugene, who supported courageously in Italy the cause of his adopted father. If the King of Naples had united with him they could together have marched on Vienna, and this audacious but at the same time perfectly practicable movement would have infallibly saved France.

These are some of the reflections I heard the Emperor make in speaking of the treachery of the King of Naples, though in the first moments, however, he did not reason so calmly. His anger was extreme, and with it was mingled grief and emotions near akin to pity: "Murat !" cried he, "Murat betray me! Murat sell himself to the English! The poor creature! He imagines that if the allies succeed in overthrowing me they would leave him the throne on which I have seated him. Poor fool! The worst fate that can befall him is that his treachery should succeed; for he would have less pity to expect from his new allies than from me."

The evening before his departure for the army, the Emperor received the corps of officers of the National Parisian Guard, and the reception was held in the great hall of the Tuileries. This ceremony was sad and imposing. His Majesty presented himself before the assembly with her Majesty the Empress, who held by the hand the King of Rome, aged three years lacking two months. Although his speech on this occasion is doubtless already well known, I repeat it here, as I do not wish that these beautiful and solemn words of my former master should be wanting in my Memoirs:

> "GENTLEMEN, Officers of the National Guard,—It is with much pleasure I see you assembled around me. I leave to-night to place myself at the head of the army. On leaving the capital I place with confidence in your care my wife and my son on whom rests so many hopes. I owe you this proof of my confidence, in return for all the innumerable proofs you have repeatedly given me in the important events of my life. I shall depart with my mind free from anxiety, since they will be under your faithful protection. I leave with you what is dearest to me in the world, next to France, and I freely commit it to your care.
>
> "It may occur that in consequence of the maneuvers I am about to make, the enemy may find the opportunity of approaching your walls. If this should take place, remember that it will be an affair of only a few days, and I will soon come to your assistance. I recommend to you to preserve unity among yourselves, and to resist all the insinuations by which efforts will be made to divide you. There will not be wanting endeavors to shake your fidelity to duty, but I rely upon you to repel these perfidious attempts."

At the end of this discourse, the Emperor bent his looks on the Empress and the King of Rome, whom his august mother held in her arms, and presenting both by his looks and gestures to the assembly this child whose expressive countenance seemed to reflect the solemnity of the occasion, he added in an agitated voice, "I confide him to you, Messieurs; I confide him to the love of my faithful city of Paris!" At these words of his Majesty innumerable shouts were heard, and innumerable arms were raised swearing to defend this priceless trust. The Empress, bathed in tears and pale with the emotion by which she was agitated, would have fallen if the Emperor had not supported her in his arms. At this sight the enthusiasm reached its height, tears flowed from all eyes, and there was not one present who did not seem willing as he retired to shed his blood for the Imperial family. On this occasion I again saw for the first time M. de Bourrienne at the palace; he wore, if I am not mistaken, the uniform of captain in the National Guard.

On the 25th of January the Emperor set out for the army, after conferring the regency on her Majesty the Empress; and that night we reached Chalons-sur-Marne. His arrival stopped the progress of the enemy's army and the retreat of our troops. Two days after he, in his turn, attacked the allies at Saint-Dizier. His Majesty's entrance into this town was marked by most touching manifestations of enthusiasm and devotion. The very moment the Emperor alighted, a former colonel, M. Bouland, an old man more than seventy years old, threw himself at his Majesty's feet, expressing to him the deep grief which the sight of foreign bayonets had caused him, and his confidence that the Emperor would drive them from the soil of France. His Majesty assisted the old veteran to rise, and said to him cheerfully that he would spare nothing to accomplish such a favorable prediction. The allies conducted themselves in the most inhuman manner at Saint-Dizier: women and old men died or were made ill under the cruel treatment which they received; and it may be imagined what a cause of rejoicing his Majesty's arrival was to the country.

The enemy having been repulsed at Saint-Dizier, the Emperor learned that the army of Silesia was being concentrated on Brienne, and immediately set out on the march through the forest of Deo, the brave soldiers who followed him appearing as indefatigable as he. He halted at the village of Eclaron, where his Majesty paid a certain sum to the inhabitants to repair their church, which the enemy had destroyed. The surgeon of this town advanced to thank the Emperor; and his Majesty examining him attentively said to him, "You have served in the army, Monsieur?"—"Yes, Sire; I was in the army of Egypt."—"Why have you no cross?"—"Sire, because I have never asked for it."—"Monsieur, you are only the more worthy of it. I hope you will wear the one I shall give you." And in a few moments his certificate was signed by the Emperor, and handed to the new chevalier, whom the Emperor recommended to give the most careful attention to the sick and wounded of our army who might be committed to his care.

> [It is known that the Emperor was not lavish in the distribution of the Cross of Honor. Of this fact I here give an additional proof. He was much pleased with the services of M. Veyrat, inspector general of police, and he desired the Cross. I presented petitions to this effect to his Majesty, who said to me one day, "I am well satisfied with Veyrat. He serves me well, and I will give him as much money as he wishes; but the Cross, never!" —CONSTANT.]

On entering Mezieres his Majesty was received by the authorities of the city, the clergy, and the National Guard. "Messieurs," said the Emperor to the National Guard who pressed around him, "we fight to day for our firesides; let us defend them in such a manner that the Cossacks may not come to warm themselves beside them. They are bad guests, who will leave no place for you. Let us show them that every Frenchman is born a soldier, and a brave one!" His Majesty on receiving the homage of the curate, perceiving that this ecclesiastic regarded him with extreme interest and agitation, consequently considered the good priest more attentively, and soon recognized in him one of the former regents of the college of Brienne. "What! is it you, my dear master?" cried the Emperor. "You have, then, never left your retirement! So much the better, since for that reason you will be only the better able to serve the cause of your native land. I need not ask if you know the country around here."—"Sire," replied the curate, "I could find my way with my eyes shut."—"Come with us, then; you will be our guide, and we will converse." The worthy priest immediately saddled his well-broken horse, and placed himself in the center of the Imperial staff.

The same day we arrived before Brienne. The Emperor's march had been so secret and so rapid that the Prussians had heard nothing of it until he suddenly appeared before their eyes. A few general officers were made prisoners; and Blucher himself, who was quietly coming out of the chateau, had only time to turn and fly as quickly as he could, under a shower of balls from our advance guard. The Emperor thought for a moment that the Prussian general had been taken, and exclaimed, "We have got that old swash-buckler. Now the campaign will not be long." The Russians who were established in the village set it on fire, and an engagement took place in the midst of the flames. Night arrived, but the combat still continued; and in the space of twelve hours the village was taken and retaken many times. The Emperor was furious that Blucher should have escaped. As he returned to headquarters, which had been established at Mezieres, his Majesty narrowly escaped being pierced through with the lance of a Cossack; but before the Emperor perceived the movement of the wretch, the brave Colonel Gourgaud, who was marching behind his Majesty, shot the Cossack dead with his pistol.

The Emperor had with him only fifteen thousand men, and they had waged an equal struggle with eighty thousand foreign soldiers. At the close of the combat the Prussians retreated to Bar-sur-Aube; and his Majesty established himself in the chateau of Brienne, where he passed two nights. I recalled during this stay the one that I had made ten years before in this same chateau of Brienne, when the Emperor was on his way to Milan with the intention of adding the title of King of Italy to that of Emperor of the French. "To-day," I said to myself, "not only is Italy lost to him, but here in the center of the French Empire, and a few leagues from his capital, the Emperor is defending himself against innumerable enemies!" The first time I saw Brienne, the Emperor was received as a sovereign by a noble family who fifteen years before had welcomed him as a protege. He had there revived the happiest remembrances of his childhood and youth; and in comparing himself in 1805 with what he had been at the Ecole Militaire had spoken with pride of the path he had trod. In 1814, on the 31st of January, the end to which this path was tending began to be seen. It is not that I wish to announce myself as having foreseen the Emperor's fall, for I did not go so far as that. Accustomed to see him trust to his star, the greater part of those who surrounded him trusted it no less than he; but nevertheless we could not conceal from ourselves that great changes had taken place. To delude ourselves in this respect it would have been necessary to close our eyes that we might neither see nor hear this multitude of foreigners, whom we had until now seen only in their own country, and who, in their turn, were now in our midst.

At each step, in fact, we found terrible proofs of the enemy's presence. After taking possession of the towns and villages, they had arrested the inhabitants, maltreated them with saber-strokes and the butt ends of their guns, stripping them of their clothing, and compelling those to follow them whom they thought capable of serving as guides on their march; and if they were not guided as they expected they killed with the sword or shot their unfortunate prisoners. Everywhere the inhabitants were made to furnish provisions, drink, cattle, forage, in a word, everything that could be useful to an army making enormous requisitions; and when they had exhausted all the resources of their victims, they finished their work of destruction by pillage and burning. The Prussians, and above all the Cossacks, were remarkable for their brutal ferocity. Sometimes these hideous savages entered the houses by main force, shared among themselves everything that fell into their hands, loaded their horses with the plunder, and broke to pieces what they could not carry away. Sometimes, not finding sufficient to satisfy their greed, they broke down the doors and windows, demolished the ceiling in order to tear out the beams, and made of these pieces and the furniture, which was too heavy to be carried away, a fire, which being communicated to the roofs of neighboring houses consumed in a moment the dwellings of the unhappy inhabitants, and forced them to take refuge in the woods.

Sometimes the more wealthy inhabitants gave them what they demanded, especially brandy, of which they drank eagerly, thinking by this compliance to escape their ferocity; but these barbarians, heated by drink, then carried their excesses to the last degree. They seized girls, women, and servants, and beat them unmercifully, in order to compel them to drink brandy until they fell in a complete state of intoxication. Many women and young girls had courage and strength to defend themselves against these brigands; but they united three or four against one, and often to avenge themselves for the resistance of these poor creatures mutilated and slew them, after having first violated them, or threw them into the midst of the bivouac fires. Farms were burned up, and families recently opulent or in comfortable circumstances were reduced in an instant to despair and poverty. Husbands and old men were slain with the sword while attempting to defend the honor of their wives and daughters; and when poor mothers attempted to approach the fires to warm the children at their breasts, they were burned or killed by the explosion of packages of cartridges, which the Cossacks threw intentionally into the fire; and the cries of pain and agony were stifled by the bursts of laughter from these monsters.

I should never end if I attempted to relate all the atrocities committed by these foreign hordes. It was the custom at the time of the Restoration to say that the complaints and narrations of those who were exposed to these excesses were exaggerated by fear or hatred. I have even heard very dignified persons jest pleasantly over the pretty ways of the Cossacks. But these wits always kept themselves at a distance from the theater of war, and had the good fortune to inhabit departments which suffered neither from the first nor second invasion. I would not advise them to address their pleasantries to the unfortunate inhabitants of Champagne, or of the departments of the east in general. It has been maintained also that the allied sovereigns and the general officers of the Russian and Prussian army severely forbade all violence in their regular troops, and that the atrocities were committed by undisciplined and ungovernable bands of Cossacks. I have been in a position to learn, on many occasions, especially at Troves, proofs to the contrary. This town has not forgotten, doubtless, how the Princes of Wurtemberg and Hohenlohe and the Emperor Alexander himself justified the burnings, pillage, violations, and numerous assassinations committed under their very eyes, not only by the Cossacks, but also by regularly enlisted and disciplined soldiers. No measures were taken by the sovereigns or by their generals to put an end to such atrocities, and nevertheless when they left a town there was needed only an order from them to remove at once the hordes of Cossacks who devastated the country.

The field of the La Rothiere was, as I have said, the rendezvous of the pupils of the military school of Brienne. It was there that the Emperor, when a child, had foreshadowed in his engagement with the scholars his gigantic combats. The engagement at La Rothiere was hotly contested; and the enemy obtained, only at the price of much blood, an advantage which they owed entirely to their numerical superiority. In the night which followed this unequal struggle, the Emperor ordered the retreat from Troves. On returning to the chateau after the battle, his Majesty narrowly escaped an imminent danger. He found himself surrounded by a troop of uhlans, and drew his sword to defend himself. M. Jardin, junior, his equerry, who followed the Emperor closely, received a ball in his arm.

Several chasseurs of the escort were wounded, but they at last succeeded in extricating his Majesty. I can assert that his Majesty showed the greatest self-possession in all encounters of this kind. On that day, as I unbuckled his sword-belt, he drew it half out of the scabbard, saying, "Do you know, Constant, the wretches have made me cut the wind with this? The rascals are too impudent. It is necessary to teach them a lesson, that they may learn to hold themselves at a respectful distance."

It is not my intention to write the history of this campaign in France, in which the Emperor displayed an activity and energy which excited to the highest point the admiration of those who surrounded him. Unfortunately, the advantages which he had obtained gradually exhausted his own troops, while only creating losses in the enemy's, which they easily repaired. It was, as M. Bourrienne has well said, a combat of an Alpine eagle with a flock of ravens: "The eagle may kill them by hundreds. Each blow of his beak is the death of an enemy; but the ravens return in still greater numbers, and continue their attack on the eagle until they at last overcome him." At Champ-Aubert, at Montmirail, at Nangis, at Montereau, and at Arcis, and in twenty other engagements, the Emperor obtained the advantage by his genius and by the courage of our army; but it was all in vain. Hardly had these masses of the enemy been scattered, before fresh ones were formed again in front of our soldiers, exhausted by continuous battles and forced marches. The army, especially that which Blucher commanded, seemed to revive of itself, and whenever beaten reappeared with forces equal, if not superior, to those which had been destroyed or dispersed. How can such an immense superiority of numbers be indefinitely resisted?

CHAPTER XXIII

The Emperor had never shown himself so worthy of admiration as during this fatal campaign in France, when, struggling against misfortunes, he performed over again the prodigies of his first wars in Italy, when fortune smiled on him. His career had begun with an attack, and the end was marked by the most magnificent defense recorded in the annals of war. And it may be said with truth that at all times and everywhere his Majesty showed himself both the perfect general and the soldier, under all circumstances furnishing an example of personal courage to such an extent, indeed, that all those who surrounded him, and whose existence was dependent on his own, were seriously alarmed. For instance, as is well known, the Emperor, at the battle of Montereau, pointed the pieces of artillery himself, recklessly exposed himself to the enemy's fire, and said to his soldiers, who were much alarmed at his danger and attempted to remove him, "Let me alone, my friends; the bullet which is to kill me has not yet been molded."

At Arcis the Emperor again fought as a common soldier, and more than once drew his sword in order to cut his way through the midst of the enemy who surrounded him. A shell fell a few steps from his horse. The animal, frightened, jumped to one side, and nearly unhorsed the Emperor, who, with his field-glass in his hand, was at the moment occupied in examining the battlefield. His Majesty settled himself again firmly in his saddle, stuck his spurs in the horse's sides, forced him to approach and put his nose to it. Just then the shell burst, and, by an almost incredible chance, neither the Emperor nor his horse was even wounded.

In more than one similar circumstance the Emperor seemed, during this campaign, to put his life at a venture; and yet it was only in the last extremity that he abandoned the hope of preserving his throne. It was a painful sacrifice to him to treat with the enemy so long as they occupied French territory; for he wished to purge the soil of France of the presence of foreigners before entering into any agreement with them whatever. And this feeling was the reason of his hesitation and refusal to accept the peace which was offered him on various occasions.

On the 8th of February, the Emperor, at the end of a long discussion with two or three of his intimate advisers, retired very late, and in a state of extreme preoccupation. He woke me often during the night, complaining of being unable to sleep, and made me extinguish and relight his lamp again and again. About five o'clock in the morning I was called again. I was almost fainting with fatigue, which his Majesty noticed, and said to me kindly, "You are worn out, my poor Constant; we are making a severe campaign, are we not? But hold out only a little longer; you will soon rest."

Encouraged by the sympathizing tones of his Majesty, I took the liberty of replying that no one could think of complaining of the fatigue or privations he endured, since they were shared by his Majesty; but that, nevertheless, the desire and hope of every one were for peace. "Ah, yes," replied the Emperor, with a kind of subdued violence, "they will have peace; they will realize what a dishonorable peace is!" I kept silence; his Majesty's chagrin distressed me deeply; and I wished at this moment that his army could have been composed of men of iron like himself, then he would have made peace only on the frontiers of France.

The tone of kindness and familiarity in which the Emperor spoke to me on this occasion recalls another circumstance which I neglected to relate in its proper place, and which I must not pass over in silence, since it furnishes such a fine example of his Majesty's conduct towards the persons of his service, and especially myself. Roustan witnessed the occurrence, and it was from him I learned the opening details.

In one of his campaigns beyond the Rhine (I do not remember which), I had passed several nights in succession without sleep, and was exhausted. The Emperor went out at eleven o'clock, and remained three or four hours; and I seated myself in his armchair, near his table, to await his return, intending to rise and retire as soon as I heard him enter, but was so exhausted with fatigue that sleep suddenly overtook me, and I dropped into a deep slumber, my head resting on my arm, and my arm on his Majesty's table. The Emperor returned at last with Marshal Berthier, and followed by Roustan. I heard nothing. The Prince de Neuchatel wished to approach and shake me that I might awake and resign to his Majesty his seat and table; but the Emperor stopped him, saying, "Let the poor fellow sleep; he has passed many nights with none." Then, as there was no other chair in the apartment, the Emperor seated himself on the edge of the bed, made the marshal also seat himself there, and they held a long conversation while I continued to sleep. At length, needing one of the maps from the table on which my arm rested, his Majesty, although he drew it out most cautiously, awoke me; and I immediately sprang to my feet, overwhelmed with confusion, and excusing myself for the liberty I had so involuntarily taken. "Monsieur Constant," the Emperor then said with an exceedingly kind smile, "I am distressed to have disturbed you. Pray, excuse me." I trust that this, in addition to what I have already related of the same nature, may serve as an answer to those who have accused him of harshness to his servants. I resume my recital of the events of 1814.

On the night of the 8th the Emperor seemed to have decided on making peace; and the whole night was spent in preparing dispatches, which on the morning of the 9th at nine o'clock were brought to him to sign; but he had changed his mind. At seven o'clock he had received news from the Russian and Prussian army; and when the Duke of Bassano entered, holding in his hand the dispatches to be signed, his Majesty was asleep over the maps where he had stuck his pens. "Ah, it is you," said he to his minister; "we will no longer need those. We are now laying plans to attack Blucher; he has taken the road from Montmirail. I am about to start. To-morrow I will fight, and again the next day. The aspect of affairs is on the point of changing, as we shall see. Let us not be precipitate; there is time enough to make such a peace as they propose." An hour after we were on the road to Sezanne.

For several days in succession after this, the heroic efforts of the Emperor and his brave soldiers were crowned with brilliant success. Immediately on their arrival at Champ-Aubert, the army, finding itself in presence of the Russian army corps, against which they had already fought at Brienne, fell on it without even waiting to take repose, separated it from the Prussian army, and took the general-in-chief and several general officers prisoners. His Majesty, whose conduct towards his conquered foes was always honorable and generous, made them dine at his table, and treated them with the greatest consideration.

The enemy were again beaten at the Farm des Frenaux by Marshals Ney and Mortier, and by the Duke of Ragusa at Vaux-Champs, where Blucher again narrowly escaped being made prisoner. At Nangis the Emperor dispersed one hundred and fifty thousand men commanded by the Prince von Schwarzenberg, and ordered in pursuit of them Marshals Oudinot, Kellermann, Macdonald, and Generals Treilhard and Gerard.

The eve of the battle of Wry, the Emperor inspected all the surroundings of this little town; and his observing glasses rested on an immense extent of marshy ground in the midst of which is the village of Bagneux, and at a short distance the village of Anglure, past which the Aube flows. After rapidly passing over the unsafe ground of these dangerous marshes, he set foot on solid ground, and seated himself on a bundle of reeds, and there, leaning against the wall of a night-hunter's hut, he unrolled his map of the campaign; and, after examining it a few moments, remounted his horse and set off at a gallop.

At this moment a flock of teal and snipe flew up before his Majesty; and he exclaimed laughingly: "Go, go, my beauties; make room for other game." His Majesty said to those around him, "This time we have them!"

The Emperor was galloping towards Anglure, in order to see if the hill of Baudemont, which is near this village, was occupied by the artillery, when the noise of cannon heard in the direction of Wry compelled him to retrace his steps; and he accordingly returned to Wry, saying to the officers who accompanied him, "Let us gallop, gentlemen, our enemies are in a hurry; we should not keep them waiting." A half hour after he was on the battlefield. Enormous clouds of smoke from the burning of Wry were driven in the faces of the Russian and Prussian columns, and partly hid the maneuvers of the French army. At that moment everything indicated the success of the plans the Emperor had formed that morning in the marshes of Bagneux, for all went well. His Majesty foresaw the defeat of the allies, and France saved, while at Anglure all were given up to despair. The population of many villages shuddered at the approach of the enemy; for not a piece of cannon was there to cut off their retreat, not a soldier to prevent them from crossing the river.

The position of the allies was so exceedingly critical that the whole French army believed them destroyed, as they had plunged with all their artillery into the marshes, and would have been mowed down by the shower of balls from our cannon if they had remained there. But suddenly they were seen to make a new effort, place themselves in line of battle, and prepare to pass the Aube. The Emperor, who could pursue them no farther without exposing his army to the danger of being swallowed up in the marshes, arrested the impetuosity of his soldiers, believing that the heights of Baudemont were covered with artillery ready to overwhelm the enemy; but hearing not a single shot in this direction, he hurried to Sezanne to hasten the advance of the troops, only to learn that those he expected to find there had been sent toward Fere Champenoise.

During this interval, a man named Ansart, a land owner at Anglure, mounted his horse, and hurried at the utmost speed to Sezanne in order to inform the marshal that the enemy were pursued by the Emperor, and about to cross the Aube. Having reached the Duke, and seeing that the corps he commanded was not taking the road to Anglure, he hastened to speak. Apparently the Emperor's, orders had not been received; for the marshal would not listen to him, treated him as a spy, and it was with much difficulty this brave man escaped being shot.

While this scene was taking place, his Majesty had already reached Sezanne; and seeing many inhabitants of this village around him, he requested some one to guide him to Fere Champenoise, whereupon a bailiff presented himself. The Emperor immediately set out, escorted by the officers who had accompanied him to Sezanne, and left the town, saying to his guide, "Go in front, monsieur, and take the shortest road." Arrived at a short distance from the battlefield of Fere Champenoise, his Majesty saw that every report of the artillery made the poor bailiff start. "You are afraid," said the Emperor to him. "No, Sire."—"Then, what makes you dodge your head?"—"It is because I am not accustomed like your Majesty to hearing all this uproar."—"One should accustom himself to everything. Fear nothing; keep on." But the guide, more dead than alive, reined in his horse, and trembled in every limb. "Come, come; I see you are really afraid. Go behind me." He obeyed, turned his horse's head, and galloped as far as Sezanne without stopping, promising himself most faithfully never again to serve as guide to the Emperor on such an occasion.

At the battle of Mery, the Emperor, under the very fire of the enemy, had a little bridge thrown over the river which flows near the town. This bridge was constructed in an hour by means of ladders fastened together, and supported by wooden beams; but as this was not sufficient, it was necessary that planks should be placed on this. None could be found, however; for those who might have been able to procure them did not dare to approach the exposed spot his Majesty occupied at this moment. Impatient, and even angry, because he could not obtain the planks for this bridge, his Majesty had the shutters of several large houses a short distance from the river taken down, and had them placed and nailed down under his own eyes. During this work he was tormented by intense thirst, and was about to dip water up in his hand to slake it, when a young girl, who had braved danger in order to draw near the Emperor, ran to a neighboring house, and brought him a glass of water and some wine, which he eagerly drank.

Astonished to see this young girl in so perilous a place, the Emperor said to her, smiling, "You would make a brave soldier, Mademoiselle; and if you are willing to wear epaulets you shall be one of my aides-de- camp." The young girl blushed, and made a courtesy to the Emperor, and was going away, when he held out his hand to her, and she kissed it. "Later," he said, "come to Paris, and remind me of the service you have rendered me to-day. You will be satisfied of my gratitude." She thanked the Emperor and withdrew, very proud of his words of commendation.

The day of the battle of Nangis an Austrian officer came in the evening to headquarters, and had a long, secret conference with his Majesty. Forty-eight hours after, at the close of the engagement at Mery, appeared a new envoy from the Prince von Schwarzenberg, with a reply from the Emperor of Austria to the confidential letter which his Majesty had written two days before to his father-in-law. We had left Mery in flames; and in the little hammock of Chatres, where headquarters had been established, there could no shelter be found for his Majesty except in the shop of a wheelwright; and the Emperor passed the night there, working, or lying on the bed all dressed, without sleeping. It was there also he received the Austrian envoy, the Prince of Lichtenstein. The prince long remained in conversation with his Majesty; and though nothing was known of the subject of their conversation, no one doubted that it related to peace. After the departure of the prince, the Emperor was in extraordinarily high spirits, which affected all those around him.

Our army had taken from the enemy thousands of prisoners; Paris had just received the Russian and Prussian banners taken at Nangis and Montereau; the Emperor had put to flight the foreign sovereigns, who even feared for a time that they might not be able to regain the frontiers; and the effect of so much success had been to restore to his Majesty his former confidence in his good fortune, though this was unfortunately only a dangerous illusion.

The Prince of Lichtenstein had hardly left headquarters when M. de Saint- Aignan, the brother-in-law of the Duke of Vicenza, and equerry of the Emperor, arrived. M. de Saint-Aignan went, I think, to his brother-in-law, who was at the Congress of Chatillon, or at least had been; for the sessions of this congress had been suspended for several days. It seems that before leaving Paris M. de Saint-Aignan held an interview with the Duke of Rovigo and another, minister, and they had given him a verbal message to the Emperor. This mission was both delicate and difficult. He would have much preferred that these gentlemen should have sent in writing the communications which they insisted he should bear to his Majesty, but they refused; and as a faithful servant M. de Saint-Aignan performed his duty, and prepared to speak the whole truth, whatever danger he might incur by so doing.

When he arrived at the wheelwright's shop at Chatres, the Emperor, as we have just seen, was abandoning himself to most brilliant dreams; which circumstance was most unfortunate for M. de Saint-Aignan, since he was the bearer of disagreeable news. He came, as we have learned since, to announce to his Majesty that he should not count upon the public mind at the capital, since they were murmuring at the prolongation of the war, and desired that the Emperor should seize the occasion of making peace. It has even been stated that the word disafection was uttered during this secret conference by the sincere and truthful lips of M. de Saint-Aignan. I cannot assert that this is true; for the door was closely shut, and M. de Saint-Aignan spoke in a low tone. It is certain, however, that his report and his candor excited his Majesty's anger to the highest degree; and in dismissing him with an abruptness he had certainly not merited, the Emperor raised his voice to such a pitch as to be heard outside. When M. de Saint-Aignan withdrew, and his Majesty summoned me to my duties near him, I found him much agitated, and pale with anger. A few hours after this scene the Emperor ordered his horse, and M. de Saint- Aignan, who had resumed his duties as equerry, approached to hold his stirrup; but as soon as the Emperor perceived him he threw on him an angry glance, made him a sign to withdraw, exclaiming loudly, "Mesgrigny!" This was Baron de Mesgrigny, another of his Majesty's squires. In compliance with his Majesty's wishes, M. de Mesgrigny performed the duties of M. de Saint-Aignan, who withdrew to the rear of the army to wait till the storm should be past. At the end of a few days his disgrace was ended, and all who knew him rejoiced; for the Baron de Saint-Aignan was beloved by all for his affability and loyalty.

From Chatres the Emperor marched on Troyes. The enemy who occupied this town seemed at first disposed to defend themselves there, but soon yielded, and evacuated it at the close of a capitulation. During the short time the, allies passed at Troyes, the Royalists had publicly announced their hatred to the Emperor, and their adherence to the allied powers, who came, they said, only to establish the Bourbons on the throne, and even had the imprudence to display the white flag and white cockade; and the foreign troops had consequently protected them, while exercising extreme harshness and severity towards those inhabitants who held contrary opinions.

Unfortunately for the Royalists they were in a very feeble minority, and the favor shown to them by the Russians and Prussians led the populace oppressed by the latter to hate the proteges as much as their protectors.

Even before the entrance of the Emperor into Troyes, Royalist proclamations addressed to the officers of his household or the army had fallen into his hands. He had showed no anger, but had urged those who had received, or who might receive, communications of this nature, to destroy them, and to inform no one of the contents. On his arrival at Troyes his Majesty rendered a decree proclaiming penalty of death against all Frenchmen in the service of the enemy, and those who wore the emblems and decorations of the ancient dynasty. An unfortunate emigre, accused before a council of war, was convicted of having worn the cross of St. Louis and the white cockade during the stay of the allies at Troyes, and of having furnished to the foreign generals all the information in his power.

The council pronounced sentence of death, for the proofs were positive, and the law not less so; and Chevalier Gonault fell a victim to his ill- judged devotion to a cause which was still far from appearing national, especially in the departments occupied by the allied armies, and was executed according to military usage.